1 0 0 % P A R I S

1 0 0 % P A R I S

There's so much to experience in Paris. Where to begin? Of course, you'll want to visit the Eiffel Tower, Notre Dame, and the Louvre. But also be sure to shop on the ritzy boulevards, drink coffee at a sidewalk café, take a walk along the Seine, dine in an authentic French bistro, or soak up the atmosphere in Montmartre. Go to the opera in the evening, or go dancing at a trendy nightclub. This guide will take you by everything you want to see in no time at all: sightseeing, shopping, culinary delights, and adventure. The easy-to-use maps will show you the way.

100% PARIS: EXPLORE THE CITY IN NO TIME!

Contents

100% Easy-to-Use

To make this guidebook easy-to-use, we've divided Paris up into six neighborhoods and provided a detailed map for each of these areas. You can see where each of the neighborhoods lies in relation to the others on the general map in the front of the book. The letters Ⓐ to Ⓩ will also let you know where to find attractions in the suburbs, hotels, and nightclubs, all described in detail later on in the guidebook.

In the six chapters that follow, you'll find detailed descriptions of what there is to do in the neighborhood, what the area's main attractions are, and where you can enjoy good food and drink, go shopping, take a walk, or just be lazy. All addresses have a number ①, and you'll find these numbers on the map at the end of each neighborhood's chapter. You can see what sort of address the number is and also where you can find the description by looking at its color:

- ⬤ = sights
- ⬤ = food & drink
- ⬤ = shopping
- ⬤ = nice to do

6 WALKS

Every chapter also has its own walk, and the maps all have a line showing you the walking route. The walk is described on the page next to the map, and it will take you past all of the most interesting spots and best places to visit in the neighborhood. You won't miss a thing. Not only will you see the most important sights, museums, and parks, but also special little shops, good places to grab lunch, and fantastic restaurants for dinner. If you don't feel like sticking to the route, you'll be able to find your way around easily with the descriptions and detailed maps.

PRICE INDICATION FOR HOTELS AND RESTAURANTS

To give you an idea of hotel and restaurant prices, you'll find an indication next to the address. The hotel prices mentioned are - unless otherwise stated - per double room per night. The restaurant prices are - unless otherwise stated - an indication of the average price of a main course.

PUBLIC HOLIDAYS

Next to the general holidays Easter, Whitsun, and Ascension Day, France observes the following public holidays:

1 January	- New Year's Day
1 May	- Labour Day
8 May	- Liberation Day (1945)
14 July	- National Holiday ('quatorze juillet')
15 August	- Assumption
1 November	- All Saints
11 November	- Liberation Day (1918)
25 December	- Christmas

DO YOU HAVE A TIP FOR US?

We've tried to compile this guide with the utmost care. However, the selection of shops and restaurants can change quite frequently in Paris. Should you no longer be able to find a certain address or have other comments or tips for us concerning this guide, please let us know. You'll find our address in the back of the book.

GEORGES

ARC DE TRIOMPH

Hotels

In addition to the well-known chains, Paris has quite a variety of excellent hotels. As in every city, the rule of thumb here is that you decide yourself just how luxurious and expensive you'd like your accommodations to be. Read on for a number of comfortable suggestions to fit every budget, you can find the letters on the general map in the front of the book.
The prices mentioned, unless specified otherwise, are per double room per night, excluding breakfast. Visit *www.francehotelguide.com* and *www.hotelstravel.com* for a further selection of hotels. For smaller budgets, explore these two very handy websites *www.hoteldiscount.fr* and *www.discountparishotels.net*.

Ⓐ Hôtel du Septième Art
Behind what looks like a typical Marais storefront is a simple and unorthodox hotel that doubles as a shop, bar and art gallery.
20 rue saint-paul, 4th arr, telephone (01) 44 54 85 00, price from €66, metro saint-paul

Ⓑ Hôtel du Quai Voltaire
Spend the night in the room where Charles Baudelaire wrote his epic poem, Les Fleurs du Mal. Room 56!
19 quai voltaire, 7th arr, telephone (01) 42 61 50 91, price from €60 per night, metro musée d'orsay

Ⓒ Hôtel Armstrong
Touristy, with a modern décor and a cyber café. Hotel Armstrong is located in the calm of a side street near the lively Bastille area.
36 rue de la croix saint-simon, 20th arr, telephone (01) 43 70 53 65, price from €75, metro père lachaise

(D) Hôtel Saint-Christophe

Charming hotel, ideally situated on a calm street. Very close to the Pantheon.
17 rue lacépède, 5th arr, telephone (01) 43 31 81 54, price from €112, metro cardinal lemoine

(E) Hôtel du Square d'Anvers

Very close to Sacré Coeur, in between Montmartre and Avenue Trudaine.
This hotel is set in a quiet and cozy garden.
6 place d'anvers, 9th arr, telephone (01) 42 81 20 74, price from €92, metro anvers

(F) Hôtel Résidence des Trois Poussins

The charm and elegance of a mansion in the old Saint-Georges district...
and close to the center of Pigalle!
15 rue clauzel, 9th arr, telephone (01) 53 32 81 81, www.les3pussins.com, price from €135, metro pigalle

(G) Villa Montparnasse

This luxurious hotel is located near Montparnasse, Parc des expositions
de la Porte de Versailles, and rue d'Alésia, known for its lively atmosphere.
2 rue boulard, 14th arr, telephone (01) 56 80 34 34, price from €189, metro denfert-rochereau

(H) Hôtel des Ecoles

Enjoy your visit to Paris by staying in a truly charming hotel. The hotel is
just a few meters from the Boulevard Saint-Germain. All rooms are ensuite
(shower/toilet), have a telephone and TV, and there is access to the Internet
provided in the hotel.
19 rue monsieur le prince, 6th arr, telephone (01) 46 33 31 69, price from €100, metro odéon

POILÂNE

LES INVALIDES

ⓘ **Normandy Hotel**

Very elegant. The hotel is close to the Opéra and the Louvre, and only a short walk from most of the interesting sights of central Paris.

7 rue de l'echelle, 1st arr, telephone (01) 42 60 30 21, price from €170, metro opéra

Ⓙ **Hôtel Villiers Etoile**

This is a three-star hotel, located only a few minutes from Paris' most prestigious boulevards. Warm hospitality.

6 rue lebouteux, 17th arr, telephone (01) 46 22 50 90, price from €183, metro villiers

Transport

Paris is the 'city of lights' and also a 'city of cars'! To ease the traffic, the city has developed a reliable (for the most part) transportation system that includes a metro, the RER (rail) and a bus line. You can access all these forms of transportations with the same ticket, which can be purchased at ticket offices or distributors in the metro, RER and bus stations.

The **metro** runs from 5.30am to 12.45am. The RER is the local **train**, but you won't need it if you stay intra-muros - within the city center. It operates from 5am to midnight. The numerous **buses** are also very convenient, and peering through their windows affords you a better opportunity to discover the city. The hours of operation depend on the area in which they run. The optimal way to travel in Paris is to choose the pass or package option that best suits your needs:

- metro tickets are good for one ride and are sold individually (€1.30) or by packs of 10 (€9.30), a 'carnet de dix'.
- for families and school groups, there is 50% discount for: children between ages 4 and 10, those who purchase a 'large family' pass, and groups of at least 10 children who are under 16 years of age.
- a weekly pass for 12 trips: you can make 12 trips (up to 2 per day for 7 days) that cover a definite destination or area. This pass can only belong to a single individual.

Paris is one of the cheapest cities in the world in terms of **taxi** prices - about €0.60 per km. It is also pretty easy to hail one of the 14,900 taxis driving in the city. The two best ways to get a taxi in Paris: hail it on the street, as long as it is more than 50 meters from a rank. If it is less than 50 meters, it can only pick you up providing there are no cabs at the rank. Or call a radio-taxi service and a taxi will then pick you up from where you are. To call a radio-taxi service from your hotel or restaurant: taxis G7, telephone (01) 47 39 47 39, taxis Bleus, telephone (01) 49 36 10 10 or Alpha-taxis, telephone (01) 45 85 85 85.

Mouffetard &
La Butte Aux Cailles

This walking tour will lead you to the fifth and thirteenth arrondissements of Paris, on the right bank of the Seine. Our chief focus will be on rue Mouffetard, the Chinese quarter and La Butte aux Cailles. Rue Mouffetard, in the fifth arrondissement, is the home of the famous Latin Quarter and the Sorbonne. The area is pretty classic and academic. Thankfully, the Mouffetard street market and the Arabic shops settled around La Mosquée de Paris have injected a certain 'je ne sais quoi' into this, one of the cleanest parts of Paris. The vast 13th arrondissement - further to the south - has several faces. It is at once 'traditional' in the northern part (an extension of the Latin Quarter), modern and cosmopolitan in its eastern section (the Bibliothèque François

Mitterrand and the Chinese district), and picturesque in the southwest (La Butte aux Cailles, a delicate vestige of a Paris that is no longer). Loved and hidden by Parisians, La Butte aux Cailles is far off the beaten touristy path. By day discover a true village lifestyle, which later morphs into a rich nightlife.

9x Musts!

Jardin du Luxembourg

Walk in Jardin
du Luxembourg.

Au Petit Suisse

Breakfast with a view
at Au Petit Suisse.

Le Panthéon

Visit Le Panthéon.

Rue Mouffetard

Shopping in
rue Mouffetard.

Cave La Bourgogne

Lunch at
Cave La Bourgogne.

**Institut du
Monde Arabe**

Visit Institut du
Monde Arabe.

Mosquée de Paris

Tea-break at
Mosquée de Paris.

Tang Frères

Shop at Tang Frères
and walk through
La Butte Aux Cailles.

**Chez Gladine &
Les Cailloux**

Dinner at Les Cailloux
or Chez Gladine.

◯ **Sights**
◯ **Shopping**
◯ **Food & drink**
● **Nice to do**

LE JARDIN DU LUXEMBOURG ①

Sights

(1) Le Palais Luxembourg was built for Marie de Medicis in 1615-1627.
The architect Salomon de Brosse, designed it as a Florentine palace, a style
favored by de Medicis. **Le Jardin du Luxembourg** (the garden) surrounds
the palace. Now here's an idea of how a true Parisian garden should be!
rue de vaugirard, 5th arr, open sunrise-sunset, metro luxembourg

(4) The Latin Quarter is also home to the **Université La Sorbonne**, the first
university founded in France (1257). It is a prestigious school due to its
rigorous academic program (and not merely because of all the cozy cafés
that surround it). If you're coming here for an education, you're guaranteed
a good one... And in between lectures, you can catch an impromptu fashion
show in the Galerie Soufflot!
12 place du panthéon, 5th arr, telephone (01) 46 34 97 00, open guided tours
mon-fri 9.30am & 2.30pm (only guided tours after reservation), admission
free, metro cluny-la sorbonne

(5) In the heart of the Latin Quarter, **Le Musée de Cluny** offers everything
you need to know about the Middle Ages. Don't miss the 'Lady and the
Unicorn' tapestries, perfect examples of the 'mille-fleurs' style. Also not
to be missed are the Gallo-Roman baths (2nd and 3rd centuries) and their
frigidarium (cold baths).
6 place paul painlevé, 5th arr, telephone (01) 53 73 78 21, open mon, wed-
sun 9.15am-5.45pm, admission €5.50, metro cluny-la sorbonne

(7) **Le Panthéon** is a masterpiece by Soufflot (1713-1780). A former church,
the Panthéon, after the French Revolution, became the necropolis of great
Frenchmen. Sixty-one 'great men' rest there, such as Voltaire, Rousseau,
Hugo, Zola, Jaurès and Moulin. This monumental structure dominates the
top of Sainte-Geneviève Mountain.
place du panthéon, 5th arr, telephone (01) 44 32 18 00, open daily winter
10am-5.30pm, summer 9.30am-6.30pm, admission €7, metro cardinal lemoine

⑰ Together with the Thermes de Cluny, the **Arènes de Lutèce** are the only remaining ruins of the Gallo-Roman era in Paris. It used to be an enormous performance space that could hold 15,000 people. Today, you can still see the location of the actors' dressing room, the stage platform and lapidary remains.

47 rue monge, 5th arr, telephone 01 45 35 02 56, open winter 8am-5.30pm, summer 8am-10pm, admission free, metro cardinal lemoine

(19) Designed by Jean Nouvel, the **Institut du Monde Arabe** has a distinctive Islamic design encapsulated by thousands of small light sensitive shutters. They contract and expand depending on how much light they are exposed to. Inside, you can explore Arab design culture as witnessed in several contemporary objets d'art, Koranic calligraphy and music. Don't forget to take the elevator to the top floor where a restaurant with a vast terrace offers one of the most beautiful views in Paris.

1 rue des fosses-saint-bernard, 5th arr, telephone insitut (01) 40 51 38 38, restaurant (01) 40 51 39 27, open institut tue-sun 10am-6pm, restaurant tue-sun 12am-6pm & 7pm-10.30pm (only after reservation), admission €4 (permanent collection), price lunch €10, diner €20, metro jussieu

(20) Would you like to know more about the wonders of nature? In the **Muséum National d'Histoire Naturelle**, you'll learn the mechanisms of evolution and the relationship between man and nature. Check-out permanent exhibition - don't be put off by some of the endangered or extinct species…a few are really strange!

57 rue cuvier, 5th arr, telephone (01) 40 79 30 00, open gallery mon, wed-sun 10am-5pm, zoo daily summer 10am-6.30pm, winter 10am-5.30pm, spring & fall 10am-6pm, admission museum €7, zoo €6, metro gare d'austerlitz or jussieu

(30) The **Manufacture des Gobelins** factory is actually a state-controlled tapestry manufactory noted for its excellent materials, dyes and workman-ship. Famous tapestries from its looms include a set based on copies of Raphael's frescoes in the Vatican and 14 great pieces commemorating the achievements of Louis XIV. Worth a visit!

42 avenue des gobelins, 13th arr, telephone (01) 44 08 52 00, open for visits tue-thu guided tours 2pm & 2.45pm, admission €8, metro gobelin

Food & drink

(2) I could not begin to explain to you what **Au Petit Suisse**, a Parisian bar tabac, has to do with Switzerland. But anyway, with its view of Jardin du Luxembourg, it's a perfect place to have breakfast. With such delicious smelling croissants, there's no better way to start a Parisian day.
16 rue de vaugirard, 6th arr, telephone (01) 43 26 03 81, open daily 7am-11.30 pm, price €10, rer Luxembourg or metre odéon

(8) Ernest Hemingway described Café des Amateurs as 'the cesspool of the rue Mouffetard'. Now it's reincarnated as **Café Delmas**, a popular place with students from the local lycées. On a sunny day, sit on the terrace overlooking the fountain.
2 place de la contrescarpe, 5th arr, telephone (01) 43 26 51 26, open daily 8am-2am, price menu €8, metro cardinal lemoine

(11) Rue Mouffetard is well known for its tasty pancakes. **Oroyona Crêperie** is maybe one of the smallest restaurants I know, but it's also where I've eaten the best pancakes in Paris! If it seems to be packed, know there is also another room upstairs.
36 rue mouffetard, 5th arr, telephone (01) 43 36 60 46, open daily 12am-midnight, metro cardinal lemoine

(12) The crowd is pretty mixed: people coming from the market, various attendants from nearby shops, students, tourists…Anybody and everybody can be found in **Le Mouffetard**, a real bar de quartier (neighborhood bar). It's a great place to observe the ebb and flow of market life.
16 rue mouffetard, 5th arr, telephone (01) 43 31 42 50, open tue-sat 7.30am-9pm, sun 7.30am-8pm, (closed july), price €10, metro cardinal lemoine

(14) At the bottom of rue Mouffetard, with a nice view of the fountain and the church St Médard, you'll appreciate the quintessentially Parisian décor and menu of **Cave La Bourgogne**. You cannot visit without sampling the Burgundy. Trust me.
144 rue mouffetard, 5th arr, telephone (01) 43 36 20 53, open tue-sun 7am-2am, price menu €14, metro censier-daubenton

Les Hauts de gramenon
Vins sobes 2000   21,50€
Côtes du Rhône Village

BLANCS:

• Touraine 1999   15€
Le Brin de chève

• Coteaux du Languedoc 1999
Les Marnes - Mas Granier 29€

㉒ The well-known restaurant **La Mer de Chine** (what some consider to be the best Chinese restaurant in Paris) serves Cantonese cuisine. You could, for example, try the 'specialité' of the cook - the sautéed tongue of duck. There are plenty of options left if duck tongue isn't your thing.
159 rue château des rentiers, 13th arr, telephone (01) 45 84 22 49, open tue-sun 12am-2.30pm, 7pm-1am, price menu lunch €13, diner €25, métro porte d' ivry

㉗ In the tiny, modest and legendary bar **Le Merle Moqueur**, the crowd (it's never empty) is young and hip. Beer, loud rock'n roll music, rum specialties - everything needed to have a good time. The popular band Mano Negra even played here…a long time ago…
11 rue de la butte aux cailles, 13th arr, telephone (01) 45 65 12 43, open daily 4pm-2am, metro place d'italie

㉘ Located in one of the nicest and most popular Parisian neighborhoods, the décor and atmosphere of **Les Cailloux** can appear to be too uptight compared with its neighbors. The restaurant, however, manages to stay interesting by offering an excellent selection of pasta and wines.
58 rue des cinq-diamants, 13th arr, telephone (01) 45 80 15 08, open tue-sat 12.30am-2.30pm & 7pm-11pm, price lunch €12,50, diner €20, metro corvisart

㉙ In the middle of this charming little autonomous village, **Chez Gladine** serves Basque specialties, as well as monumental salads and heaps of potatoes - just like home cooking. The place is crowded. Don't expect to linger over a three-hour dinner, people are waiting to take your seat!
30 rue des cinq diamants, telephone (01) 45 80 70 10, open daily 12am-4pm & 7pm-2am, price menu lunch €9.50, diner 15, metro corvisart or place d'italie

Shopping

(3) Close to Jardin du Luxembourg, these designers of preserved and dried flowers are doing an amazing job! There is such a delicateness to the floral sculptures of **Les Couturiers de la Nature** that you'll be afraid to touch them! Fortunately, these artist are pragmatic too: their masterpieces can last for more than 5 years!
16 rue de vaugirard, 6th arr, telephone (01) 43 26 18 25, open mon-sat 11am-7pm, rer luxembourg

(6) **Arkham** has plenty of toys and comic books specially imported from the US weekly. Find the X-men for your nephew. Purchase a glorious comic book. A little America in Paris.
15 rue soufflot, 5th arr, telephone (01) 40 51 82 55, open mon-sat 10am-8pm, sun 2pm-7pm, rer Luxembourg

(9) Sylvie Bouyer has opened a boutique under her own label **Balthazar.f**. What is particularly interesting about her work is her ability to create modern styles while using traditional luxurious fabrics. In addition to her own collection, she carries many big names in French ready-to-wear.
9 rue blanville, 5th arr, telephone (01) 43 25 04 24, open tue-sat 11am-7.30pm, metro cardinal lemoine

(10) So many 'arty' eyeglasses, but which one fits me best? No worries, just enter the shop of **Soly Amor**, the first French visagiste! Instead of just telling you which pair of glasses to choose, the attendant will be more than happy to also share his knowledge about the intricacies of 'the face'.
6 rue du pot de fer, 5th arr, telephone no, open mon-sat 3pm-8pm, metro cardinal lemoine

(13) Entering **L'Epée de Bois** is a real pleasure. First, because owners Rémi and Geneviève are so very kind. Second, because you'll have entered into the colorful and wonderfully imaginative world of 0 to 10 year olds. You'll fall for the hand-crafted toys. I loved the little red firetruck built by a Corsican artist.
12 rue de l'epée de bois, 5th arr, telephone (01) 43 31 50 18, open mon 1.30pm-7.30pm, tue-sat 10.30am-7.30pm, sun 11am-1.30pm, metro cardinal lemoine

...et John Galliano

Mouna Ayoub et Karl Lagerfeld

Mathieu Demy, Sarah Barsand et Marco Prince

...umbach

Jean-Marc Loubier (Céline), Olga Schmitt (Citizen K International), Anna Mouglalis et un ami

Monica Pillosio (Citizen K International), Sarah Paruitti et ... Lignelli (Christian Dior)

...et Kappauf

Guy Pierlaert, le papa de Pravda et d'Groon

Federico Cimatti, Olga Schmitt et Gilles Rosier (Gilles Rosier et...

...Tornatti (Paco Ki), Vincent

Bénédicte Luridy Sfrombart (L'Oréal Produits de Luxe) et Monsieur, Monsieur et Madame Joël Ponte et Odile Roujol (Lancôme)

Olga Schmitt, Mouna Ayoub incognito et Ali Madhavi

...et Chaubin (Citizen K international)

Monica Pillosio (Citizen K International) et Jeremy Scott

Olympia Le Tan

SOLY AMOR ⑩

...Citizen K International), Cyril Lefèvre et Jean-Baptiste Perrin

Benoît Béthume, Monica Pillosio, Cyril Lefèvre et un ami, Laurent Gonsalez (agence ...pique et un), Citizen K International, Olga Schmitt, Armande Altaï et Stéphane Arbteux

⑮ When describing **Maison Franco-Orientale**, its friendly owners compare the boutique to a 'souk' (a Moroccan market) and to Ali Baba's Cavern! This shop specializes in Afghan jewelry, tea glasses and many other products from countries that span from Morocco to India. I couldn't help but eye an amazing collection of North African shoes, 'babouches'.

19 rue daubenton, 5th arr, telephone (01) 40 46 78 10, open daily 10.30am-8pm, metro monge

(18) Near the university, located far from the fashionable streets of rue Fbg St Honoré, and rue Royale, **Asphalte** found its own identity and quickly became one of the most creative design boutiques in the city. The gallery-shop attracts hip customers coming to find original and exclusive pieces from both famous and unknown designers.

35 rue jussieu, 5th arr, telephone (01) 43 29 99 59, open tue-sun 11am-2pm & 2.30pm-7pm, metro jussieu

(23) The two brothers of **Tang Frères** come from Laos and have turned a former French railway warehouse into Europe's largest Asian market. The area has become a tourist spot, attracting shoppers from the Paris suburbs, French provinces and other countries. Go inside. The smells in the shop are overwhelming. Memorable!

48 ave d'ivry, 13th arr, telephone (01) 45 70 80 00, open tue-sun 9am-7.30pm, metro porte d'ivry

(24) Not surprisingly, the house designer at **Indigo** prefers to create clothes using Chinese indigo blue. You can find house creations mixed in with other designs coming from all over Asia...When I was in the minuscule shop last time, a female customer insisted that I note in this guide that only regular customers come there. Well, I did it!

44 avenue d'ivry, center commercial oslo, 13th arr, telephone (01) 45 85 16 16, open tue-sun 11am-7pm, metro porte d'ivry

(25) **AO-TA** is a place I found by chance. Now I want you to see it for yourself. Take the escalator at number 44 Avenue d'Ivry. It'll lead you to the so-kitsch-that-it's-beautiful Olympiades shopping mall. Once inside, make a right at the BNP bank. There you'll discover AO-TA and its great choice of fabrics and Vietnamese 'prêt-à-porter'.

44 avenue d' ivry, center commercial oslo, 13th arr, telephone (01) 53 82 11 48, open tue-sun 11am-7pm, metro porte d'ivry

Nice to do

(16) **La Mosquée de Paris** (the Paris Mosque) was built in 1922 as a memorial to Muslims who died in World War I. It is open to visitors, and so I invite you to spoil your body and your soul in the hammam (Turkish Bathhouse) and prayer space. Don't forget, shoes must be removed at the entrance. There's also a restaurant and an excellent tearoom, which sells a variety of Arabic pastries and other delights. A must.
2 place du puits de l'ermite, 5th arr, telephone (01) 45 35 97 33, open restaurant daily 12.30am-3pm & 7.30pm-10.30pm, salon de thé daily 9am-11pm, price €12, metro place monge

(21) Paris is known for its artists and its intellectuals. If you fancy yourself one of the latter, visit the four towers of **Bibliothèque François Mitterrand**, which houses the Bibliothèque Nationale and the Bibliothèque de France. The books found in these hallowed library halls cover all fields of scholarship.
9 boulevard vincent auriol, entrance quai françois mauriac, 13th arr, telephone (01) 53 79 59 59, open for public mon 2pm-7pm, tue-sat 9am-8pm, sun 12am-7pm, admission €3, metro bibliothèque françois mitterrand

(26) The famous French puppet Guignol was created between 1810 and 1812 by Laurent Mourguet. In 1820, Mourguet created the first traveling puppet troop, **Théâtre Guignol Lyonnais Du Parc De Choisy**, which toured Southern France. Don't miss this opportunity to experience a wonderful theatrical performance. Bring your children.
parc de choisy, in front of 149 de l'avenue de choisy, 13th arr, telephone (01) 43 66 72 39, open wed, sat-sun 3.30pm, closed dec-feb, admission €2.50, metro place d'italie

HEATRE D UIGNOL

Mouffetard &
La Butte Aux Cailles

Don't do this walking tour on Monday - nearly everything is closed! Exit the Luxembourg metro station and happen upon the Jardin du Luxembourg ①, where you'll find Parisians performing their daily stroll through the park. Leave the park via rue de Vaugirard ② ③ and head towards the Sorbonne ④ and Musée de Cluny ⑤. Next continue via the rue Saint-Jacques to rue Soufflot ⑥. Make your way towards Le Panthéon ⑦, the necropolis of great Frenchmen! Sainte-Geneviève hill, on which the Pantheon rests, got its name from the legendary heroine who saved Paris from the invasion of barbarians in the 5th century. Next, continue to Place de la Contrescarpe, which is dominated by a fountain and the terrace of Café Delmas ⑧ ⑨. Stroll through rue Mouffetard ⑩ ⑪, one of the oldest streets in Paris. Here you'll find a lively market, facing the Saint-Médard church ⑫ ⑬ ⑭. Head left via rue Daubenton ⑮ to rue Monge. Enjoy the divine Mosquée ⑯ and walk northwards via the century-old ruins of Arènes de Lutèce ⑰ and the shop Asphalte ⑱ towards the Seine to Institut du Monde Arabe ⑲. Together with the mosque these two edifices symbolize the Arab culture that holds dominance in this neighborhood. Feel free to follow along the Seine, passing the Jardin des Plantes to the Musée National d'Histoire Naturelle ⑳ and further on to the Bibliothèque François Mitterrand ㉑. Walk behind the library towards the rue de Tolbiac. Take a right and eventually find yourself in a kind of Chinatown. Follow this route to the rue du Château des Rentiers ㉒ and turn left. Continue by rue de Regnault towards the right until avenue d'Ivry, and turn right. On this street you'll discover many products imported directly from Asia ㉓ ㉔ ㉕. The puppet theater, Guignol ㉖, further up the street, is a must for children. Turn left at the theater onto rue du Moulinet. In this little neighborhood, La Butte aux Cailles, you'll find lots of little picturesque streets, filled with bars ㉗ and restaurants ㉘ ㉙ popular with young Parisians. For one more cultural lesson, walk towards Place d'Italie and turn left on avenue des Gobelins to visit the Manufacture des Gobelins ㉚.

2

reminiscent of the Paris of old, but because it is busting at the seams with people and cars, it is difficult to enjoy the exquisite architecture. It is a relief then to arrive on the two islands of Ile de la Cité and Ile Saint-Louis. Both are wonderfully unique, but for my money, Ile Saint-Louis is more attractive with its small picturesque streets.

9x Musts!

Tournesol

Breakfast at
café Tournesol.

Tour Montparnasse

The view from the top
of Tour Montparnasse.

**Saint-Germain-
des-Prés**

Shopping at Saint-
Germain des-Prés.

Bar du Marché

Lunch at Bar du Marché.

Notre Dame de Paris

A walk through Saint-
Michel to Notre Dame.

Le Flore en l'Ile

High tea at
Le Flore en l'Ile.

Berthillon

Ile-Saint-Louis and
a Berthillon ice-cream.

Calife

A dinner cruise
on Calife.

**Mezzanine
de l'Alcazar**

Mezzanine de l'Alcazar.

 Sights
 Shopping
Food & drink
 Nice to do

EGLISE SAINT-SULPICE ⑪

Sights

(2) There are myths and a whole culture built around the underground world of Paris, the **Catacombes**. Look down and see bones from the old cemeteries of Paris. There are some other illegal entrances to the 'combs, used by Parisians. Private underground parties? You didn't read about it here.

1 place denfert-rochereau, 14th arr, telephone (01) 43 22 47 63, open tue-fri 2pm-4pm, sat-sun 9am-11am and 2pm-4pm, admission €5, metro denfert-rochereau

(5) With its panoramic view from the 56th and 59th floors, **La Tour Montparnasse** is a classic 20th century monument: 686 feet high, featuring the fastest lift in Europe, which makes it to the top in 38 seconds! On the 56th floor there are exhibitions, a photo series capturing the history of Paris and a video room.

rue de l'arrivée, 15th arr, telephone (01) 45 38 52 56, open daily 9.30am-10pm, admission €7.60, metro montparnasse bienvenue

(11) Full-time construction on **Eglise Saint-Sulpice** did not start until the 16th century and took 135 years to be completed. As a result, the interior of the church reflects different periods of architecture. For a bit of mystery, note the straight line on the floor made of copper, called 'meridian'. No one seems to know what it's for...

place saint-sulpice, 5th arr, open daily 8.30am-7.30pm, admission free, metro saint-sulpice

LA TOUR MONTPARNASSE ⑤

㉒ Originally, **Ile de la Cité** was two uninhabited islands : Ile aux Vaches (Island of Cows) and Ile Notre-Dame, which belonged to the cathedral. In the early 17th century, the two islands were joined by Christophe Marie and were entirely built up by 1664. The island is now the police headquarters and is clogged with traffic jams...a sad destiny.

ile de la cite, 4th arr, metro cité

㉓ **Sainte-Chapelle** was built under Saint-Louis, the king of France, to house the Crown of Thorns and a fragment of the True Cross (of Jesus Christ). Its construction was completed in 1248. The cathedral includes two chapels: the low chapel intended for the servants of the King and the high chapel reserved for the royal family. The stained-glass windows, restored in the 19th century, date from the 13th century and cover a surface of 2,034 square feet. They recall scenes from Old and New Testaments.
4 boulevard du palais, 1st arr, telephone (01) 53 73 78 51, open daily 9.30am-5pm, admission €5.50, metro cité

㉔ Contrary to its name, **Le Pont Neuf** (the New Bridge) is the oldest (and the longest) bridge in Paris. Construction on it began in 1578 in order to create an easier path for the king between Louvre Palace and the St-Germain-des-Prés church. It was inaugurated in 1607 by Henri IV.
le pont neuf, 1st arr, metro pont neuf

㉕ **La Conciergerie** became the first prison in 1391. Danton was one of many who stayed in the gallery, and today you can visit the space and see a reconstruction of the prison cells of his time. The windows of the gallery look on to a square where the wives and mothers of the prisoners gathered to walk.
1 quai de l'horloge, 1st arr, telephone (01)53 73 78 50, open daily apr-sep 9.30am-5pm, oct-mar 10am-5pm, admission €5.50, metro cité

㉖ A gothic masterpiece. **Notre Dame de Paris**, conceived by Maurice de Sully, was built between the twelfth and fourteenth centuries (1163-1345). The interior is richly decorated with stained-glass windows and a multitude of sculptures. It also has one of the biggest organs in the world. Forget the hunchback. Did you know that Napoléon was crowned emperor here in 1804?
place du parvis de notre dame, 4th arr, telephone (01) 42 34 56 10, open daily, 7.45am-7.45pm, admission €5.50, metro cité

Food & drink

(4) **Le Tournesol** is a new bar profiting from the bustling neighborhood in which it is located. Actors from nearby theatres like to pop in and mix with the young, easygoing, Parisian clientele. Great atmosphere, friendly hosts.
9 rue de la gaîté, 14th arr, telephone (01) 43 27 65 72, open daily 8am-2am, metro gaîté

(14) **Chez Georges** is a tiny bar known all over the city (and particularly by students) for its excellent and inexpensive wines. The atmosphere is warm and familial. In fact, if you're alone and want to practice your French, it's a great place to socialize.
11 rue des canettes, 6th arr, telephone (01) 43 26 79 15, open tue-sat 12am-2am, metro odéon

(16) You haven't experienced Saint-Germain-des-Prés until you've spent an hour sipping coffee at **Les Deux Magots**. You can almost taste the café's history. Picasso and André Breton were habitués, as was the existentialist clan.
170 blvd saint-germain, 6th arr, telephone (01) 45 48 55 25, open daily 8am–2am, price menu €30, metro saint-germain-des-prés

(17) I hadn't been to **La Palette** for a while, and when I visited recently, I saw him again - legendary waiter Jean-François. Same beard, same unwelcoming face. La Palette, an old French-style café, never changes. That's why it's such a great place.
43 rue de seine, 6e arr, telephone (01) 43 26 68 15, open mon-sat 8am-2am, price €11, metro odéon

(18) Comfortable and stylish, **Mezzanine de l'Alcazar** has become one of the best places to listen to house music in Paris. The restaurant, a bit expensive, is less interesting. You'll find more yuppies at l'Alcazar than clubbers…but who cares, the music is excellent.
62 rue mazarine, 6th arr, telephone (01) 53 10 19 99, open daily12am-3pm & 7pm-2am, price lunch €15, diner €40, metro odéon

16 LES DEUX MAGOTS

⑳ Rue de Buci is a busy shopping street where you'll find all kinds of goodies and tasty foods to satisfy your cravings. The terrace of **Bar du Marché** is an excellent place to people-watch. At lunch time, I advise you to order the 'croque-monsieur' (a hot ham and cheese sandwhich), served with a friendly smile by waiters donning berets…A must!
75 rue de seine, 6th arr, telephone (01) 43 26 55 15, open daily 8am-2am, price €10, metro odéon

㉑ After the success of the **Bar Les Etages** in Le Marais, a second Bar les Etages settled here. The concept is more or less that you order your drinks and tapas on the first level and then take them back to your seat on one of the upper floors.
5 rue de buci, 6th arr, telephone (01) 46 34 26 26, open daily 11am-2am, metro odéon

㉗ After crossing the bridge, you arrive on Ile Saint-Louis. The outdoor terrace of **Le Flore en l'Ile** faces the rear of Notre Dame. The view speaks for itself.
42 quai d'orléans, 4th arr, telephone (01) 43 29 88 27, open daily 8am-2am, price menu €40, metro cité

㉘ Ice-cream in France does not enjoy quite the same status as gelato in Italy… **Berthillon** is the exception to the rule. They serve the most delicate and succulent sorbets in Paris. THE Parisian ice-cream!
31 rue saint-louis-en-ile, 4th arr, telephone (01) 43 54 31 61, open gelato wed-sun10am-8pm, salon de dégustation wed-fri 1pm-8pm, sat-sun 2pm-8pm, metro saint-michel

Shopping

(1) Like the markets of Montreuil or St Ouen, you'll find second-hand clothes and a wide variety of 'knickknacks' in **Le Marché aux Puces de Vanves**. This one, however, is particularly rich in antiques (there are some good deals to be had!), old jewelry and furniture. Note that aside from the metro, bus n°58 can also take you back to the city center.
avenue georges-lafenestre, 14th arr, open sat-sun 7am-5pm, metro porte de vanves

(6) To make your trip perfect, while at a café, request your croque-monsieur to be made with bread from **Poilâne**. This Parisian bakery offers all sorts of delicious breads, which are baked to the specifications of old secret family recipes. I usually buy the country, nut and raisin breads…Delicious !
8 rue du cherche-midi, 6th arr, telephone (01) 45 48 42 59, open mon-sat 7.15am-8.15pm, metro sèvres-babylone

(7) After a long history of designing swimwear, **Eres** has applied their aesthetic to a line of fine lingerie. Eres celebrates women's bodies using sensual designs crafted in materials as light and delicate as a fine soufflé.
4 rue du cherche midi, 6th arr, telephone (01) 45 44 95 54, open mon-sat 10.30am-7pm, metro sèvres-babylone

(8) **Stealth** offers an avant-garde mix of menswear and womenswear, an array of jewelry, and - a collection of Star Wars figures! Check out these brands : Evisu, Duffer, Aem'kei.
42 rue du dragon, 6th arr, telephone (01) 45 49 24 14, open mon 2pm-7.30pm, tue-sat 10.30am-7.30pm, metro saint-germain-des-prés

(9) It's true that shoes speak more about a person than anything else. So, go ahead and make the most of your first impression. Hipsters must visit **Shoe Bizz**. It's got shoes to please well-heeled men and women alike. It certainly helps me put my best foot forward.
42 rue du dragon, 6e arr, telephone (01) 46 05 05 80, open mon 2pm-7.30pm, tue-sat 10.30am-7.30pm, metro saint-germain-des-prés

(10) Parisian women are Agnès b women. Comfortable and stylish, her clothes are defintely staples for the female inhabitants of this city. And now, men also have their own Agnès b store - **Agnès b homme** ...We deserve to be stylish too, I guess.

10 rue du vieux colombier, 6e arr, telephone (01) 45 49 02 05, open mon-sat 10am-7pm, metro saint-sulpice

(12) Already well known in London and Tokyo, **Muji** offers functional objects for the home or office, as well as an array of beauty accessories. All products come in wood, plastic, aluminium and/or craft board. Simplicity and functionality prevails.
27 rue saint-sulpice, 6th arr, telephone (01) 46 34 01 10, open mon-fri 10am-7.30pm, sat 10am-8pm, metro st-sulpice

(13) If you think like I used to think, **Dr. Martens** only offers up boots for tough guys and gals. Surprise yourself (like I did) by pushing open the doors of its concept boutique and discover a range of cool accessories and fantastic bags.
23 rue des canettes, 6th arr, telephone (01) 55 42 62 12, open tue-sat 10.30am-7.30pm, metro saint-sulpice

(15) **Onward** has clothing, bags, shoes, jewlery and lingerie by known designers such as Thimister and Helmut Lang. The clean and modern boutique is unassuming, and many people make the mistake of passing it by. You, however, now have no excuse to miss it!
147 boulevard saint-germain, 6th arr, telephone (01) 55 42 77 55, open mon, sat 11am-7pm, tue-fri 10.30am-7pm, metro saint-germain-des-prés

(19) All of the interior designs by Finnish architect Alvar Aalto produced by Artek since 1935 are available at **Torvinoka**. Also discover the unique collection called 'Art de la Table'.
4 rue cardinale, 6th arr, telephone (01) 43 25 09 13, open mon2pm-7pm, tue-sat 10am-7pm, metro saint-germain-des-prés

(30) **Les Bouquinistes** have been peddling books on the sides of the Seine since the construction of the Pont-Neuf. Over the following years, however, the government tried to rid the area of them. In 1891, they were officially authorized to operate only if they agreed to respect the location and set-up their stalls in such a way as to allow passer-bys to see the river and its banks.
both sides of the seine, metro pont neuf

Nice to do

③ **Théâtre Montparnasse**'s exquisite exterior fronts rue de la Gaîté. The theatre opened in 1772, and Harold Pinter, Arthur Miller, Ewald Von Kleist and Arrabal all performed here in the sixties. Today, Myriam de Colombi directs the company. Guaranteed entertainment!
31 rue de la gaîté, 14th arr, telephone (01) 43 22 77 74, metro edgar-quinet

㉙ Jump aboard the **Calife** for a unique adventure! The Seine, under the gracious beauty of Notre-Dame, will gently lead you past the most romantic sights in the city…These amazing views don't come cheap, but what do you care?
5 quai de montébéllo, 5th arr, telephone (01) 43 54 50 04, cruise apr-sep tue-sat 8.30pm, price menu €50, metro cité

THÉÂTRE MONTPARNASSE ③

Rive Gauche

Begin at the Porte de Vanves metro station and continue via boulevard Brune towards the flea market ❶. Walk further on the boulevard, and turn left onto avenue Jean Moulin. Continue via avenue de Géneral le Clerc to the Catacombes ❷. Follow along the cemetery via rue de Froideveaux towards the charming rue de la Gaite ❸ ❹, to discover the imposing Tour Montparnasse ❺. Go along Place du 18 Juin 1940 to the most important street in this neighborhood, the rue de Rennes, where you'll find a large variety of clothing and accessories stores. Don't forget to weave in and out of the delightful side streets, where you'll find all the trendy boutiques ❻ ❼ ❽ ❾. Famous labels like Agnès b ❿ and others ⓬ ⓭ ⓮ ⓯ are also located in this neighborhood nearby Place Saint-Sulpice. On Saint-Sulpice, pay a visit to the Saint-Sulpice church ⓫. Via the grand boulevard Saint-Germain you'll reach the café of Saint-Germain-des-Prés, Les Deux Magots ⓰, where Vian, Jean-Paul Sartre and Simone De Beauvoir were regulars. Turn right to reach the little streets around the abbey of Saint-Germain to find lots of cool shops and restaurants ⓱ ⓲ ⓳. This neighborhood is also teeming with high quality galleries. The nicest restaurants can be found on rue de Seine ⓴ and rue de Buci ㉑. Further up, via the market, rue Saint-André des Arts will lead you to Saint-Michel, where you'll find even more restaurants. Walk to the quay of the Seine to admire the beauty of Ile de la Cité ㉒. Cross over Pont Saint-Michel to reach the island ㉓ ㉔ ㉕. You'll notice the extremely long line to enter Notre Dame ㉖. Did you know that just before the entrance of Notre Dame there is a spot called '0 km'? All of the main road distances in France are calculated from this point. The other island, Ile Saint-Louis, is even more beautiful, filled with gorgeous houses. You have an exceptional view of Paris from number 45 on the Quai de Bourbon ㉗ ㉘, If you decide to visit Paris in spring or summer, then you can end the day with a romantic boat ride on the Calife ㉙ ㉚.

3

visiting some fantastic celebrity bars and restaurants. Elite spots like Man Ray and Buddha Bar have managed to attract a young - and wealthy - clientele. It won't come as a surprise that you shouldn't go out in this area without being properly dressed. Men, however, should avoid the tie - it's a bit too serious. Welcome to the neighborhood of the 'Bohemian Bourgeois'!

9x Musts!

Ladurée

Breakfast at Ladurée on les Champs Elysées.

Arc de Triomphe

Visit the Arc de Triomphe.

Rue Faubourg Saint-Honoré

High fashion on rue Faubourg Saint-Honoré, then Village Royale.

L'Absinthe

Lunch at l'Absinthe.

Blvd. Haussmann

Shopping at Le Printemps and Galeries Lafayette on blvd. Haussmann.

Les Invalides

Walking through the gardens of Les Invalides.

Musée Jacquemard-André

Tea at Musée Jacquemard-André.

Korova

A trendy dinner at Korova.

Man Ray

See and be seen at Man Ray.

 Sights

 Shopping

 Food & drink

 Nice to do

Sights

(1) The **Champs Elysées** is rich in history. 'La plus belle avenue du monde' (the most beautiful avenue in the world) is, for the French, a symbol of luxury and patriotism. Today, the area is a concentration of a little bit of everything: monuments, fast food joints, hundreds of shops, clubs, tourists, pickpockets, policemen, businessmen, homeless people, etc. In fact, everybody feels comfortable here. On this avenue, life's best and the worst have learned to coexist…
champs elysées, 8th arr, metro charles-de-gaulle-etoile

(2) Commissioned in 1806 by Napoleon, some time after his victory in Austerlitz, the **Arc de Triomphe** wasn't completed until 1836. The four huge relief sculptures at the base of the four pillars commemorate the Triumph of 1810. Journey to the top see a grand perspective of the Champs Elysées.
place charles de gaulle, 8th arr, telephone (01) 55 37 73 77, open daily apr-sep 10am-11p, oct-may 10am-10.30pm, admission €7, metro charles-de-gaulle-etoile

(8) The **Musée Jacquemard-André** was originally the private residence of avid collectors who devoted their entire lives to amassing their art collection. It's a luxurious space, and the salon-de-thé is one of the most beautiful in Paris, with its Brussels tapestries and Tiepolo ceiling. I assure you, they serve a great brunch on Sundays!
158 boulevard haussman, 8th arr, telephone (01) 42 89 04 91, open daily 11am-6pm, admission €8, metro saint-philippe du roule.

(14) In 1814, Louis XVIII announced that **La Madeleine** should be transformed into a church. In 1837, however, it was nearly selected to be the first railway station of Paris! In 1842, it was indeed consecrated as a church, and today, concerts are held there several times a week, usually in the evening. Enjoy a splendid view of Paris that travels along rue Royale, through Concorde Square, across the Seine to the National Assembly.
place de la madeleine, 14, rue de surène, 8th arr, telephone (01) 44 51 69 00, open mon-sat 7am-7pm, sun 7am-1.30pm & 3.30pm-7pm, admission free, metro madeleine

(18) **Place de la Concorde**, situated along the Seine, is the largest square in Paris. Its historical significance is grisly, as it served as the location where Louis XVI was guillotined. Today, this once bloody square is teeming with bloody traffic!

place de la concorde, 1st arr, metro concorde

(24) As the former home of the kings of France, the **Musée du Louvre** is the largest museum in the world. Its collections are divided among seven departments: Oriental antiques, Egyptian antiques, Greek, Etruscan and Roman antiques, Paintings, Sculptures and Objets d'Art from the Middle Ages to 1850. If you have the dogged ambition to study each masterpiece, then I advise you, bring a tent!

34-36 quai du louvre, 1st arr, telephone (01) 40 20 51 51, open mon, wed 9am-9.45pm, thu-sun 9am-6pm, admission €.50, metro louvre

(25) The **Musée d'Orsay** was built in 1977 and opened to the public in December 1986. It is known worldwide for its famous impressionists collection. Aside from its sculptures, paintings, and graphic and decorative arts, the museum also exhibits collections of furniture, architecture and photography.

1 rue de bellechasse, 7th arr, telephone (01) 40 49 48 14, open tue-wed, fri-sat 10am-6pm (jun 18th-sep 29th open at 9am), thu 9am-9.45pm, sun 9am-6pm, admission €7, metro solferino

(26) In 1670, Louis XIV founded **Les Invalides**. On April 3, 1861, Napoléon I was laid to rest in the crypt under the golden cupola. Today, it's a popular place for tossing around a Frisbee. How times have changed...

129 rue de grenelle, 7th arr, telephone (01) 44 42 37 72, open mon-sat 10am-4.45pm, sun 10am-5.15pm, admission €6, metro invalides

a collection of books by artists

(28) **Le Pont de l'Alma** was built in 1970-74 and became world-(in)famous recently as the location of the tragic death of Princess Diana in 1997. The site has become a memorial ground, and the copy of the Liberty Flame, built atop the tunnel, burns in memory of her. Formerly filled with flowers, poems and messages, it has since been cleaned and is no longer filled with crowds of mourners.

le pont de l'alma, 8th arr, metro alma marceau

(29) Certainly one of the most innovative cultural and intellectual creations in Paris within the two last years! **Palais de Tokyo** is not your typical 'silence is golden' museum. This is a 21st century experience where you can walk, talk and indeed interact as freely as you like. Drink, eat and talk with the artist, he'll be around...

13 avenue du président wilson, 16th arr, telephone (01) 47 23 54 01, open tue-sun 12am-midnight, admission €5, metro iéna

(30) I can safely say **La Tour Eiffel** is the most famous monument in the world. Built by Gustave Eiffel in 1889 for the World Fair, it was a shining star from the beginning. Information about the tower can be found on all floors. The restaurant Le Jules Verne is on the second floor. Tip: If you want to spend New Year's Eve there, book 3 years in advance!

champs de mars, 7th arr, telephone (01) 44 11 23 23, open daily jan 1st-jun 13th & sep 1st-dec 31st 9.30am-11pm, jun 14th-aug 31st 9am-midnight, admission to 1st floor €3.70, 2nd floor €6.90, top €9.90, metro bir hakeim

Food & drink

(3) Louis Ernest Ladurée opened his first bakery in 1862 at 16, rue Royale in Paris. In September of 1997, a new boutique, **Ladurée**, was opened on the Champs-Elysées. While there are so many delicious products to choose from, try the macaroons, the house specialty, famous everywhere in Paris and all over the world!

75 avenue des champs-elysées, 8th arr, telephone (01) 40 75 08 75, open daily 7.30am-1am, metro george v

(4) Dinner and a show all rolled into one. **Lido** provides an entire evening's worth of entertainment, and chef Paul Bocuse's food is simply divine. If you'd prefer to sample another restaurant and come here just for the show, that's cool too. Order champagne and enjoy.

116 bis avenue des champs elysées, 8th arr, telephone (01) 40 76 56 10, open shows sun-thu 9.30pm, fri-sat 9.30pm &11.30pm, admission show €90, price diner €45, metro george v

(5) **Man Ray**. Johnny Depp and Sean Penn own the place… So, you can understand why it is currently one of Paris's trendiest restaurants among the rich and beautiful. The food blends French and Asian cuisines. At night funky house, trip hop and techno, will rock you and the Parisian jet set crowd…

34 rue marbeuf, 8th arr, telephone (01) 56 88 36 36, open daily 12am-3pm, 8pm-2am (fri until 5am), price lunch €15, diner menu €55, metro franklin d. roosevelt

(6) **Korova** is for dining and people watching. The chef, Hermé, is known as a ceaseless innovator who likes to mix tastes. Korova serves a mouth-watering blend of fantastic foods in a super-stylish setting.

33 rue marboeuf, 8th arr, telephone (01) 53 89 93 93, open mon-fri 9am-2am, sat-sun 10am-2 am, price menu €70, metro champs-elysées

(7) **L'Appart** is located in a duplex, and its name hearkens to its cozy atmosphere, reminiscent of a personal dining room or library. In the basement, a large bar with cocktails is presided over by professional 'mixologists'. The succulent cuisine…French, of course.

9 rue du colisée, 8th arr, telephone (01) 53 75 16 34, open tue-sat 12am-1.30am, zo-ma 12am-12.30am, metro franklin roosevelt

(16) Enjoy your lunch on the terrace of **Florès**. It's even warmed up for you for winter lunches alfresco. Among the pastries and salads served are tarte tatin, lemon tarts and chocolate tarts. They also make a wickedly thick hot chocolate served plain. Come on!

village royale, 25, rue royale, 8th arr, telephone (01) 40 17 02 19, open mon-sat 8am-8pm, price lunch €10, metro madeleine

(17) Push open the big door of the **Buddha Bar** and enter another world. A space where tables are arranged around an enormous statue of the Buddha. You're transported inside a Tibetan temple smelling of incense. You're in the world of models and actors…A bit pricey, but it's worth the journey!

8 rue boissy d'anglas, 8th arr, telephone (01) 53 05 90 00, open daily 12am-3pm & 6pm-2am, price menu €80, metro concorde

(21) You're hungry or just want a rest. You crave a quiet, sunny and cordial spot. Then you'll enjoy the fine cuisine and charm of **L'Absinthe**.

24 place du marché st-honoré, 1st arr, telephone (01) 49 26 90 04, open mon-fri, sun 12am-3pm & 7pm-midnight, sat 7pm-midnight, metro tuileries

(23) Want a delicious 'chocolat chaud' (hot chocolate), walk to **Angelina** under the arcades of rue de Rivoli. Their 'chocolat chaud l'Africain' is a well-known Parisian taste-sensation. Expensive, but a grand old place to have afternoon break when it's cold!

226 rue de rivoli, 1st arr, telephone (01) 42 60 82 00, open daily 9am-7pm, metro tuileries

(31) **Soleil d'Est** is worth knowing about because it is the first Chinese restaurant to receive a Michelin star. As a small boy in Shangai, Mr Chen, the chef, cooked for his family. Today he cooks for you and, the food is quite simply amazing.

15 rue du theatre, 8th arr, telephone (01) 45 79 34 34, open mon-sat 12am-11pm, price menu €40, metro bir hakeim.

Shopping

(9) A visit to France always provides a great opportunity to discover and bring home some rare bottles of wine. At the wine shop **Caves Augé**, you'll receive professional advice. Opened in 1850, it is one of the oldest wine shops in Paris. Aside from me, Marcel Proust was also one of the regular customers.

116 boulevard haussmann, 8th arr, telephone (01) 45 22 16 97, open mon 1pm-7.30pm, tue-sun 9am-7.30pm, metro st-augustin

(10) **Citadium** is a place where customers can find the newest and most stylish brands of active wear. Note the rare Nike watches at the entrance on your left. This place is so trendy that DJs spin records here on Saturday afternoons.

55-56 rue caumartin, 9th arr, telephone (01) 55 31 74 00, open mon-wed, fri-sat 9am-7pm, thu 9am-9pm, metro havre-caumartin

(11) If I had a dime for every time a lost tourist has asked me where the **Galeries Lafayette** are… Mix shopping and culture. Galeries Lafayette has a beautiful glass and steel dome, and an Art Nouveau staircase built in 1912 by the architect Cahnautin.

40 boulevard haussmann, 9th arr, telephone (01) 42 82 34 56, open mon-wed, fri-sat 9.30am-7pm, thu 9.30am-9pm, metro havre-caumartin

(12) Just in front of Citadium, **Printemps de l'Homme** offers a wide range of designer labels for men. There is also a salon for men, offering manicures and backrubs. On the top floor, in The World Bar, designed by Paul Smith, you can sip a soda while enjoying the view.

64 boulevard haussmann, 9th arr, telephone (01) 42 82 50 00, open mon-sat 9.30am-7pm, thu 9.30am-10pm, metro havre-caumartin

(15) Established in 1886, **Fauchon** is considered to be one of the greatest luxury food stores in Paris. There is a patisserie, a cellar for fine wines, a tearoom and restaurant, and a traiteur that caters private dinner parties.

26 place de la madeleine, 8th arr, telephone (01) 47 42 60 11, open mon-sat 9.30am-7pm, metro madeleine

(19) The hip space of **Bleu comme Bleu** unites clothes, shoes, a restaurant and a hair salon. On the ground floor you'll find fashion brands for men and women, plus baby wear. Upstairs, visit the men's and women's hair salon, color studio and beauty treatment area. This beauty ain't cheap though. It's one of the most expensive 'salons de beauté' in Paris!
2 rue de castiglione, 1st arr, telephone (01) 53 81 85 53, open mon-sat 9.30am-7pm, metro tuileries

(20) As a great trend maker, wherever Rei Kawakubo opens a new space, it causes a sensation. The Japanese designer, with her pink windowed boutique, has revolutionized things again by totally changing the concept of the perfume store. In the window of **Comme Des Garçons Parfum** you can only catch a glimpse of the Eau de Cologne - and that's all. Curious enough to enter?
23 place du marché saint-honoré, 1st arr, telephone (01) 47 03 15 03, open mon-sat 11am-7pm, metro pyramides

(22) **Colette** was the first 'concept boutique' in Paris. Here find Nike sneakers, cool watches, jewelry, music, art, whatever. Everything here is limited edition. Downstairs, discover the famous restaurant/Water Bar, which features hundreds of different kinds of water (try a glass of Australian rain). Colette has given shopping in Paris new meaning and is now a marketing icon.
213 rue saint-honoré, 1st arr, telephone (01) 55 35 33 90, open mon-sat 10.30am-7.30pm, metro tuileries

(27) Enjoy stinky cheese? Soft cheese? Whatever 'cheeses' you, I suggest you sit above the cheese shop **Androuët**, in the restaurant, and sample some of their 200 varieties. One of the most famous cheese shops in Paris!
83 rue saint-dominique, 7th arr, telephone (01) 45 50 45 75, open mon-sat 10.30am-7.30pm, closed in august, metro la tour-maubourg

Nice to do

⑬ Built between 1862-1875, the **Opéra Garnier**'s architect, Charles Garnier, created a performance hall of 11,000 square meters, with a vast stage to accommodate up to 450 artists. Marc Chagall painting the colorful frescoes on the ceiling in 1964. For me, seeing a ballet in this space is truly a breathtaking experience.

place de l'opéra, 9th arr, telephone (01) 40 01 22 63, open daily summer 10am-6pm, winter 10am-5pm, metro opéra

·CHORÉGRAPHIE·

Rive Droite

Outside Charles de Gaulle metro, you'll arrive directly on the Champs Elysées ① with the Arc de Triomphe ②. Further up on the Champs Elysées is Ladurée ③, whose doors open early, making it the ideal address for breakfast. This is also the neighborhood for night owls. Therefore, make it back in the evenings to visit the area's many 'restoclubs' ④ ⑤ ⑥ ⑦ for dining or dancing. Go to the endless shops found on rue du Faubourg Saint-Honoré and boulevard Hausmann ⑨ ⑩. Or have a cup of tea in the Musée Jacquemard-André ⑧. If you're short on time, there are shopping centers ⑪ ⑫ where you can find great deals. Break at the café -restaurant on the top floor and enjoy the view on the Opéra Garnier ⑬ and La Madeleine ⑭. Walk via rue Scribe along the Opéra toward Madeleine to the many delicatessens ⑮, or stop off at Florès ⑯ on one of the most atmospheric squares in Paris. Admire the majestic view of rue Royale, or in the direction of La Madeleine look towards Place de la Concorde ⑰ ⑱. Have you worked up an appetite? Then walk via rue de Rivoli left to rue de Castiglione ⑲ and right to rue de Faubourg Saint-Honoré, towards Place du Marché Saint-Honoré. Not far from here, near the shops ⑳ and many terraces ㉑, you'll find places to lunch. Make sure that you return to Faubourg Saint-Honoré to visit Colette ㉒ the first 'concept store' in the city. Want warm chocolate milk? Head to Angelina ㉓. Museum-lovers can get their fix at the Louvre ㉔ or across the Seine at the Musée d'Orsay ㉕. Walk via rue de Bellechasse right to rue Saint-Dominique to Les Invalides ㉖. Don't forget to stop by the delicious cheese shop ㉗. Go left onto avenue Bosquet towards the water. Pay your respects to the late Princess Diana at Pont de l'Alma ㉘. Also, make sure you visit Palais de Tokyo ㉙. A perfect way to start the evening is with a visit to the Eiffel Tower ㉚ for a splendid view of Paris. Afterwards dine in one of the trendy restaurants in the neighborhood. Perhaps try Soleil d'Est ㉛.

1. Champs Elysées
2. Arc de Triomphe
3. Ladurée
4. Lido
5. Man Ray
6. Korova
7. L'Appart
8. Musée Jacquemard-André
9. Caves Augé
10. Citadium
11. Galeries Lafayette
12. Printemps
13. Opéra Garnier
14. La Madeleine
15. Fauchon
16. Florès
17. Buddha Bar
18. Place de la Concorde
19. Bleu comme Bleu
20. Comme Des Garçons Parfum
21. L'Absinthe
22. Colette
23. Angelina
24. Louvre
25. Musée d'Orsay
26. Les Invalides
27. Androuët
28. Pont de l'Alma
29. Palais de Tokyo
30. Eiffel Tower
31. Soleil d'Est

○ Sights
○ Food & drink
◉ Shopping
● Nice to do

Montorgueil, Le Marais & Le Bastille

Creative types have been settling in the Montorgueil neighborhood, in the 2nd arrondissement, for quite a long time. Mainly a pedestrian zone, Montorgueil offers a large selection of restaurants and cafés. These effervescent streets abound with crowded terraces, on which you are invited to enjoy an endless array of dishes. Montorgueil street, famous for its small trade, is the nerve center of this area. Les Forum des Halles, in the center of Paris, attracts a host of people, as an area overrun with shops and also as a location where several metro lines and the RER intersect. Le Marais in Paris' 4th arrondissement has been predominately Jewish since the thirteenth century. Today,

an established gay community has transformed it of one of the city's most fashionable quarters. Finally, we'll tour the 11th arrondissement, principally in the Bastille quarter. The most famous landmark is Place de la Bastille. For Parisians, it is a popular nighttime destination. The area is always packed in the evening, so much so, that the district seems to be spilling over into surrounding neighborhoods.

9x Musts!

La Grappe d'Orgueil

A croissant and coffee
at La Grappe d'Orgueil.

Le Centre Pompidou

Art at Le Centre
Pompidou.

Kiliwatch

Shopping in the trendy
Killiwatch.

Café de l'Industrie

Tea break at
Café de l'Industrie.

Le Marais

Shopping in Le Marais.

Rue des Rosiers

A falafel lunch on
rue des Rosiers.

Musée Picasso

Visit the Musée Picasso.

Bofinger

Dinner at Bofinger,
a classic Parisian
brasserie.

Café du Trésor

Have a drink at
Café du Trésor.

- ◯ Sights
- ● Shopping
- ◯ Food & drink
- ● Nice to do

Sights

(5) In 1183, Philippe Auguste built two huge buildings called **Les Halles** as the location for an enormous Parisian market place. A few decades ago, the market had to be moved to the south of Paris. In its place, Forum des Halles, a commercial shopping center, opened in 1979. It is a popular meeting place for Parisians. An institution.
101 porte berger, 1st arr, telephone (01) 44 76 96 56, ope mon-sat 10am-7.30pm, metro châtelet-les-halles

(9) **Le Centre Pompidou** was recently renovated in 1999. The Musée National d'Art Moderne remains the heart of the center, with an enlarged exhibition space and 1,400 works on show (instead of the former 800). In addition, there is also a spectacular restaurant on the top floor.
19 rue beaubourg, 4th arr, telephone (01) 44 78 12 33, open mon, wed-fri 12am-10pm, sat-sun 10am-10pm, metro rambuteau-hôtel de ville

(11) This tower, **La Tour Saint-Jacques**, is the last gothic vestige and former bell-tower of the Saint-Jacques-de-la-Boucherie church, so-named because it was erected in a neighborhood of butchers. Pilgrims making their way to Saint-Jacques-de-Compostelle (a popular pilgrimage dedicated to Saint-Jacques) used to gather at this point. Today, it serves quite a different purpose as a meteorological station. Here, scientists measure the air quality and pollution level in Paris.
place du châtelet, 4th arr, metro châtelet

(12) The **Hôtel de Ville de Paris** has been the center of political life in Paris for centuries. During the Middle Ages, people were executed on the square in front of the city hall. It was then rebuilt after the 16th century original was set fire to during the 1870 Parisian revolution. No worries today, however. It is now relatively tranquil and decorated with fountains.
place de l' hôtel de ville, 4th arr, telephone (010 42 76 54 04, open only for guided tours after reservation, admission free, metro hôtel de ville

㉓ **LA PLACE DES VOSGES**

⑳ **Synagogue Agudath Hakehilot** was built in 1914 by Hector Guimard, the Art Nouveau architect famous for the green entrances to Paris' metros. Guimard's American wife was Jewish, and with the rise of Nazism, they left France for the United States. The synagogue was blown apart by the Germans, but has since been restored. It is now a national monument.
10 rue pavée, 4th arr, telephone (01) 48 87 21 54, metro saint-paul

㉑ The **Musée Picasso** presents Pablo Picasso's works and personal collection, received by the State after his death. The Hôtel Salé, in which it's housed, was built between 1656 and 1659 for Pierre Aubert, a salt (salé) tax collector. It's a special place for me, reader - it was the first museum I visited when I moved to Paris!
hôtel salé, 5 rue de thorigny, 3rd arr, telephone (01) 42 71 25 21, open wed-mon 9am-5.30pm, admission €5.50, metro saint-paul

㉓ **La Place des Vosges** lies in the heart of the fashionable Marais district, not far from the new Bastille opera. King Henri IV commissioned it at the beginning of the 17th century, and the result boasts a brick and stone architecture unique in Paris. It also features an homogeneous square design and lovely arcades. Many illustrious Frenchmen have lived there, including the writer Victor Hugo, whose museum rests at number 6.
place des vosges, 4th arr, metro st paul

① **LA GRAPPE D'ORGUEIL**

Food & drink

(1) Montorgueil street is full of attractive terraces - great when the sun is shining. If you can manage to find a seat at **La Grappe d'orgueil**, enjoy a coffee. The owner is kind, making this a great place to start your day.
5 rue des petits carreaux, 2nd arr, telephone (01) 40 13 00 17, open tue-sat 10am-8pm, sun 10am-4pm, price €10, metro sentier

(7) There is a very small Asian community in the Arts et Métiers neighborhood. At number 16 Rue Au Maire, you'll find my favorite 'canteen' **Salon de thé Weng Zhou**. It's a tiny and friendly Asian restaurant serving up an inexpensive meal and a healthy dose of Eastern culture.
16 rue au maire, 3rd arr, telephone (01) 42 74 05 09, open mon-sat 10am-10.30pm, price €6, metro arts-et-métiers

(10) The décor of **Georges** is perfectly in keeping with the contemporary art that surrounds it. Also hoping to be seen is the fashionable crowd that frequents the place. Hyper-modern cutlery, sandblasted glass tables and a terrific terrace with unobstructed views over all of Paris complete the stellar effect. The food is a bit expensive and the portions are small, but apparently, no one cares.
centre pompidou, place georges pompidou, 4th arr, telephone (01) 44 78 47 99, open kitchen mon, wed-sun 11.30am-2.30pm & 6pm-midnight, price menu €70, metro châtelet

(13) If it ain't broke, don't fix it. But if it is broke…You'll be amazed at what can be found in the basement of BHV. Just follow your nose to the **Bricolo Café**. Frequented by handymen who shop in the makeshift BHV workshop, Bricolo offers excellent coffee and pastries.
60 rue de rivoli, 4th arr, telephone (01) 42 74 90 00, open mon-tue, thu-sat 9.30am-7pm, wed 9.30am-10pm, metro hôtel de ville

(14) The **Open Café** has become a mecca for gay boys meeting up before heading off into the night. It is always crowded and bubbling over with energy. The management also runs the Open Bar Coffee Shop at No 15.
17 rue des archives, 4th arr, telephone (01) 42 72 26 18, open daily 11am-2am, metro hôtel de ville

(17) The classic **Le Petit Fer à Cheval** café has a perfect terrace for watching the Marais crowd pass by. The name of the café comes from its horse-shoe-shaped bar fashioned out of zinc...Before leaving, have a look at the futuristic iron bathrooms!
30 rue vieille du temple, 4th arr, telephone (01) 42 72 47 47, open daily 9am-1am, price menu €28, metro hôtel de ville

(18) The colorful and hip **Café du Trésor** is always full. Well known for it's 'early hours' (starts at 9.30pm), it has a wonderful mix of DJs. The crowd is sometimes so young that those over 24 may feel a bit 'over the hill'. Don't let that stop you though - it's great fun!
57 rue du trésor, 4th arr, telephone (01) 44 78 06 60, open daily 11am-2am, metro saint-paul

(24) The first **Bofinger** was a small bar that served draught and charcuterie. Legend has it that Berlioz used to come here to order his favorite dish - lobster mayonnaise. It is now a huge brasserie, and I recommend the plates of fresh seafood. Not extremely expensive, Bofinger is certainly worth a visit. Bookings should be made as early as possible!
3 rue bastille, 4th arr, telephone (01) 42 72 87 82, open daily 12am-3pm & 6pm-1am, price menu lunch €25, diner €30, metro bastille

(25) The Bastille area is the most crowded place to go out... it seems as if everyone in Paris and its suburbs fill the area each Saturday night! For some quiet, **Café de l'Industrie** is hidden in a small street and is in fact closed on Saturdays. A peaceful Parisian ambiance...
16 rue saint-sabin, 11th arr, telephone 47 00 13 53, open sun-fri 10am-2am, price menu €20, metro bréguet-sabin

(28) Whether it's a blazing summer night or in the dead of a blistery winter, instinctively bodies rub together upon entering **Sanz Sans**! The music varies, but the groove is always right. The crowd is cosmopolitan, young, and friendly. During the day, food is served in a more relaxed atmosphere.
49 rue du faubourg saint-antoine, 11th arr, telephone (01) 44 75 78 78, open daily 12am-2.30pm & 6pm-11.30pm, price lunch €10, diner €25, metro bastille

㉙ Doing your groceries at the Marché d'Aligre, and wondering why so many people are standing outside the **Le Baron Rouge bar** that early in the morning? Meet the regulars - folks who know the awesome effects that a good glass of wine served with a few oysters has on the soul! A good mood is de rigueur here.

1 rue théophile roussel, 12th arr, telephone (01) 43 42 54 65, open tue-thu 10am-2pm & 5pm-10pm, fri-sat 10am-10pm, sun 10am-3pm, price snacks €7, metro ledru-rollin

Shopping ✎

(2) Everybody agrees that **Kiliwatch** is a must. It houses the most expansive collection of secondhand clothing in all of trendy Paris. The secret to its success is its creative mix of used clothes with new Diesel, Levi's, G-Star and other street-smart brands. You can also pick-up the latest issues of hip magazines.
64 rue tiquetonne, 4th arr, telephone (01) 42 21 17 37, open mon 2pm-7pm, tue-sat 11am-7pm, metro étienne marcel

(3) Very close to Place des Victoires and the Galeries Vivienne, **Kokon To Zai** has all the trendiest clothes one could want. But then again, I expect no less from a London export.
48 rue tiquetonne, 2nd arr, telephone (01) 42 36 92 41, open daily 11am-7pm, metro étienne marcel

(4) **Barbara Bui**'s terminally hip boutique features both sensual and modern clothes from the most Western of the Eastern designers. Bui's self-named café is two doors down, at the corner of rue Française. The café is as minimalist as hyper-fashion necessitates it should be. For fashion victims.
23 rue étienne marcel, 1st arr, telephone (01) 40 26 43 65, open mon 1pm-7pm, tue-sat 10.30am-7.30pm, metro étienne marcel

(6) **Etam** has merged its brands together into one superstore. Shoes, accessories and fashion collections are housed on the second floor, with a hairdresser on the third. You'll find 'Tammy' (Etam's clothes for children) on the fourth floor and a bar/ restaurant on the fifth. The clothes won't change your life, but it's good to pick up the necessities...
67-73 rue de rivoli, 4th arr, telephone (01) 44 76 73 73, open mon-wed, fri-sat 10am-8pm, thu 10am-9pm, metro pont neuf

(15) Are you a Levi's addict? Levi's has opened this unofficial outpost to sell its limited edition and vintage jeans. **Nim** (short for denim) also sells limited edition Adidas and exhibits works by young artists.
16 rue du bourg tibourg, 4th arr, telephone (01) 42 77 19 79, open tiue-sat 1pm-8pm, metro hôtel de ville

④ BARBARA BUI

⑲ A temple to the Fashion Gods, **L'Eclaireur** is a one-stop-shop for edgy designs by Prada, Dries Van Noten, Ann Demeulemeester, Jil Sander, Martin Margiela and Helmut Lang, all proffered in warm surroundings - a pleasant respite from the steely minimalism that pervades other high-fashion boutiques.
3-ter rue des rosiers, 4th arr, telephone (01) 48 87 10 22, open mon-sat 11am-7pm, metro saint-paul

㉒ **L'Habilleur** offers an impressive stock of last season's clothing collections at up to 50% off! It is a prime destination for fashion-hungry men and women. Look for designs by Olivier Strelli, Martine Sitbon, Patrick Cox, Dice Kayek…
44 rue de poitou, 3rd arr, telephone (01) 48 87 77 12, open mon-sat 11am-8pm, metro saint-sebastien froissart

㉖ **Gravity Zero II** has collections of clothing and accessories created by independent designers. In contrast to the cold, minimalist fashion boutiques that are ever so popular in the city, Gravity Zero II has been able to mix contemporary décor with a warm setting. See what I mean for yourself.
1 rue keller, 30, rue de Charonne, 11th arr, telephone (01) 49 23 41 75, open mon 2pm-7pm, tue-thu 11am-1pm & 2pm-7.30pm, fri-sat 11am-7.30pm, metro bastille

㉚ **Marché d'Aligre** is one of Paris' flea markets offering fabrics, antiques and thousand of different objects. Located in the pleasant setting of Place d'Aligre, it is also one of Paris' most agreeable open-air markets. Definitely one of the liveliest places in Paris on Sunday.
place d'aligre, 12th arr, open daily from 7.30am-12.30pm, metro ledru rollin

Nice to do

(8) All those éclairs-au-chocolat and scoops of ice cream going to your hips? Want to lose it before the trip home? Then you need the best sports club in town. Paris' best trainers work at **Espace Vit'Halles**. Most of them have won prestigious European and world competitions.
48 rue rambuteau, 3rd arr, telephone (01) 42 77 21 71, open mon-fri 8am-10.30pm, sat 10am-7pm, sun 10am-6pm, metro rambuteau

(16) At **Athletic world**, you can lift weights, enjoy a hot sauna, experience uva, request a massage, and relax in a hammam. Daily prices are around €16.77. Enjoy! For men only.
20 rue du bourg-tibourg, 4th arr, telephone (01) 42 77 19 78, open tue-thu 12am-2am, fri-mon 4pm-2am, metro hôtel de ville

(27) The **Opéra Bastille** was opened by President François Mitterrand on July 13, 1989. Today it primarily hosts large-scale classics like Carmen (the world's most popular opera), Tosca, or Rigoletto. In front, la Colonne de Juillet marks the site of the prison known as the Bastille, which was stormed by the mob in 1789.
place de la bastille, 12th arr, telephone (01) 44 73 13 00 (reservations), admission €9,15, metro bastille

Montorgueil, Le Marais & Le Bastille

Begin at Sentier metro station. Walk via rue Réaumur and turn right onto rue des Petits Carreaux for morning coffee ①. Find great window-shopping on the following streets: rue Tiquetonne ② ③, rue Etienne Marcel, Place des Victoires. Many renowned designers such as Barbara Bui ④ are situated in this neighborhood. And if you are a shoe-hound, then this is the neighborhood for you. Best to avoid the crowded Les Halles ⑤ on Saturdays. Visit on the other days, just to say you've been. Continue along rue des Halles to rue de Rivoli ⑥, boulevard de Sébastopol and rue de Turbigo to reach the Arts et Metiers neighborhood ⑦. Go to rue Beaubourg and turn right onto rue Rambuteau ❽ and continue on to the Centre Pompidou ⑨ ⑩. Go via rue le Boucher to rue Saint-Martin - a fantastic street filled with secondhand stores. Further on stands La Tour Saint-Jacques ⑪ and the terrific Le Marais neighborhood. Lovers of techno-music and street wear will enjoy shopping in these streets ⑫ ⑬ ⑭ ⑮. This is a trendy gay neighborhood filled with fashionable stops ❶⑥ ⑰ ⑱. And rue des Rosiers ⑲ is the famous Jewish street in Paris. Visit the Synagogue ⑳ and the local pastry shops or falafel houses. Follow along rue des Payenne, where you'll find even more trendy shops. Keep an eye on your wallet here! Continue on to rue de Thorigny to visit the beautiful Musée Picasso ㉑, and travel further via rue du Poitou ㉒ and rue de Turenne to the lovely Place des Vosges ㉓. Continue on to rue des Tournelles, rue Bastille ㉔, boulevard Richard Lenoir, and right onto rue Saint-Sabin ㉕, rue Keller and rue de Charonne, all perfect shopping streets ㉖. And for the evening? Visit rue de Lappe and rue du Faubourg Saint-Antoine to party all night long ㉗. Naturally, you can always attend the Opéra ㉘, for a more cultural evening. You can also find the label Aligre ㉙ ㉚ in this neighborhood.

1. La Grappe d'Orgueil
2. Kiliwatch
3. Kokon To Zai
4. Barbara Bui
5. Les Halles
6. Etam
7. Salon de Thé Weng Zhou
8. Espace Vit'Halles
9. Centre Pompidou
10. Georges
11. Tour Saint-Jacques
12. Hôtel de Ville de Paris
13. Bricolo Café
14. Open Café
15. Nim
16. Athletic world
17. Le Petit Fer à Cheval
18. Café du Trésor
19. L'Eclaireur
20. Synagogue Agudath Hakehilot
21. Musée Picasso
22. L'Habilleur
23. Place des Vosges
24. Bofinger
25. Café de l'Industrie
26. Gravity Zero II
27. Opéra Bastille
28. Sans Sanz
29. Le Baron Rouge
30. Marché d'Aligre

- ○ Sights
- ○ Food & drink
- ● Shopping
- ● Nice to do

Belleville & Ménilmontant

The village of Belleville, formed in the Middle Ages around several large Parisian abbeys, acquired its name in the 18th century, probably derived from 'Belle Vue' (Beautiful Sight). Today, Belleville is a working-class neighborhood populated mostly by immigrants. On this walk, you will discover the eastern portion of Paris, a popular area filled with a variety of historical landmarks, which form an integral part of daily life (parks, a cemetery, flea markets…). The tour will also lead you to Ménilmontant, the soul of which

is rue Oberkampf. Its cafés are essentially Parisian during the day, brimming with local folk, like young Parisians playing chess or holding the occasional poetry reading over a cup of mint tea. The evening scene is always hectic, and the bars are packed every night!

9x Musts!

Le Galopin

Breakfast at Le Galopin, place Sainte-Marthe.

Parc des Buttes Chaumon

Parc des Buttes Chaumont.

Mouzaïa & Belleville

Visit the Mouzaia area and the high hills of Belleville.

Rital et Courts

An Italian lunch at Rital et Courts.

Parc de Belleville

Parc de Belleville.

Musée Edith Piaf

Shop in Oberkampf and visit the Edith Piaf Museum.

Café Charbon

A break at Café Charbon.

La Boulangerie

Dinner at la Boulangerie… no worries; it's not a bakery!

La Flèche d'Or

La Flèche d'Or Café is the place to go but closes at 2am.

 Sights
 Shopping

 Food & drink
 Nice to do

MOUZAÏA ④

Sights

(2) **Georges Lardennois street** is unknown even among Parisians.
I found it by chance once when I was going to the nearby Parc des Buttes
Chaumont. This area is pretty exceptional because you have an amazing
view from Sacré Coeur, which you don't get from the top of Parc de Belleville.
rue georges lardennois, 19th arr, metro colonel fabien

(3) **Le Parc des Buttes Chaumonts** was once a quarry. Napoleon III ordered
Haussmann to supervise the transformation from bland landmark into a park
of beauty and distinction. The park has an expansive lake overlooked by a
promontory, embellished by the 'Temple de Sybille', a replica of Tivoli.
Amidst 'ancient' trees and statues, this is definitely a place for picnics!
rue botzaris, rue manin, avenue simon-bolivar, 19th arr, metro buttes-chaumont

(4) The name of the **Mouzaïa Quarter** is derived from an infamous battle
in Algeria in 1839 and is formed by a few streets between rues Mouzaïa,
General Brunet and Miguel Hidalgo. Because of the area's structural
foundation, large, heavy buildings are not allowed in this charming quarter,
leaving instead at neighborhood filled with small houses and quaint gardens.
No two houses are alike.
rues mouzaïa, rue general brunet en rue miguel hidalgo, 19e arr, metro botzaris

(7) While walking along rue des Cascades, take note of the numerous stone
structures resembling tiny houses. Called '**Regards**', they were actually
control stations for the aqueducts that were built when the water from this
once fertile area was channeled downhill to serve the needs of Paris.
11 rue des cascades, rue de savie, 20th arr, metro pyrénées

LE PARC DES BUTTES CHAUMONTS ③

⑧ Castel, born November 15, 1688 in Montpellier, was a strong opponent of Sir Isaac Newton's views on science. But the house that bears his name, **Villa Castel**, is actually better known because it is where François Truffaut performed scenes from the famous French film Jules and Jim. Don't hesitate to open the wrought-iron gate that guards the entrance of the villa to have a peek.

16 rue de transvaal, 20th arr, metro pyrénées

(10) Offering a brilliant panoramic view of Paris, **Le Parc de Belleville** integrates many elements that recall the history of the neighborhood: there used to be artificial caves, but today you'll find free flowing cascades and water basins, which hearken to the existence of subsoil waters. Note that the waterfall is over 100 yards long and so is the longest in Paris!
rue piat, rue des couronnes, rue julien-lacroix, rue jouye-rouve, 20th arr, metro pyrénées

(11) The **Maison de l'air** ('House of air') exhibits anything that relates to the air: windmills, airplanes, seeds, studies on the Earth's atmosphere, breathing etc. After visiting this museum, you'll be an amateur meteorologist after having handled weather-related instruments, learned cloud recognition and discovered how to interpret satellites images.
parc de belleville, rue piat, 20th arr, telephone 01 43 49 28 02, open oct-mar tue-sun 1.30pm-5pm, apr-sept mon-fri 1.30pm-5.30pm, sat-sun 1.30pm-6.30pm, admission €3.35, metro pyrénées

(23) You'll need to make an appointment to visit the free apartment museum, **Musée Edith Piaf**, which was founded in 1977. Actually famous singer Edith Piaf never lived in this neighborhood as an adult, but she did spent time here in her childhood. You'll discover a beautiful China collection, decorative arts, jewelry, furniture, paintings, photography, sculpture, textiles, stamps, and letters.
5 rue crespin du gast, 11th arr, telephone (01) 43 55 52 72, open by appointment mon-wed 1pm-6pm, thu 10pm-12pm, admission free, metro ménilmontant

(27) The most famous cemetery in Paris is **Cimetière du Père Lachaise**, final resting place of Oscar Wilde, Marcel Proust, Colette, Edith Piaf, Jim Morrison and Frédéric Chopin. Chestnut trees line some of the avenues, giving you the relaxed feel of a country park!
principal entrance, boulevard de ménilmontant, telephone (01) 55 25 82 10, open mon-sat 8am-5.45pm, sun 9am-5.45pm, admission free, metro père lachaise

㉗ CIMETIÈRE DU PÈRE LACHAISE

Food & drink

(1) Travel to Marseille without leaving the 10th arrondissement. On days when the sun is starting to shine again, the ambiance of place Sainte-Marthe, where **Le Galopin** is located, feels like the aforementioned Mediterranean city. Enjoy the soft light and quiet... A great place for breakfast!
34 rue ste-marthe, 10th arr, telephone (01) 53 19 19 55, open tue-fr 12am-2.30pm & 8pm-11pm, sat 8pm-11pm, price menu €17, metro colonel fabien

(9) **Rital et Courts**, in the heart of Belleville, is extremely enjoyable. It gathers together people from the neighborhood and creative professionals such as producers, decorators, sound engineers, etc... From 3.30pm to 7pm and from midnight to 2am, short movies and documentaries are screened...accompanied by delicious Italian food.
1-3 rue des envierges,20th arr, telephone (01) 47 97 08 40, open tue-sat 10am-midnight, sun 10am-6pm, price lunch €10, diner €20, metro pyrénées

(12) **Chez Ramona** is a bit like home: the TV is on, grannies chat away, music fills the room, customers sing... But the highlight is the food - huge portions of delicious paella, filled with meats and seafood made by Ramona and her daughter (also named Ramona). The Spanish wine has to be tested too. Spain in the midst of Paris.
17 rue ramponneau, 20th arr, telephone (01) 46 36 83 55, open tue-sun 7pm-2am, price €12, metro belleville

(13) **Aux Folies**' décor dates to the Thirties. Each day, a cosmopolitan mix of customers made up of Chinese men and women, Jews, Arabs, and French men and women show up, representative of Belleville's ethnic diversity. The atmosphere is always congenial, and talking to your neighbor is encouraged!
8 rue de belleville, 20th arr, telephone (01) 46 36 65 98, open daily 6.30am-midnight, metro belleville

㉒ **Le Café Charbon** began as a music hall, in which, according to the rumor, Mistinguett and Maurice Chevallier made their débuts. It is now a trendy place that serves a terrific Sunday brunch.
114 rue oberkampf, 11th arr, telephone (01) 41 20 70 95, open daily 9am-2am, price €10, metro ménilmontant

㉔ In the purest tradition of the Parisian brasserie, **Le Soleil**, is a popular café with a huge terrace of plastic tables and chairs set out on the sunny sidewalk…The place to be in summer for sure, if you'd like to feel as if you've drifted off to the South of France!
14 boulvard ménilmontant, 20th arr, telephone (01) 46 36 47 44, open daily 8am-2am, metro ménilmontant

㉕ A bit lost behind the better known bar Le Soleil and far from the crowded rue Oberkampf, you'll still find **Lou Pascalou**, well-known for serving up an ambiance reminiscent of Ménilmontant ten years ago. That means cheap beer, not many tourists and a bohemian atmosphere. A place for Parisian nostalgia.
14 rue des panoyaux, 20th arr, telephone (01) 46 36 78 10, open daily 9am-2.am, metro ménilmontant

㉖ As its name indicates, **La Boulangerie** used to be a bakery. The lovingly restored interior features a mosaic floor, murals and old-style wooden tables. Find a great selection of meats and fish, fresh ingredients prepared with care and innovative cooking. A perfect location.
12 rue des panoyaux, 20th arr, telephone (01) 43 58 45 45, open sun-fri 12am-2.30pm & 7.30pm-midnight, price €15, metro ménilmontant

㉘ **La Flèche d'Or** is the old, no-longer-used station of the 'Petite Ceinture', the historic train line that went all around the city. Today, in the same spot, you can brunch, have a drink, dine and dance. Every evening you'll stumble upon concerts, films and, every Sunday at 5pm, a dance hall.
102-bis rue de bagnolet, 20th arr, telephone (01) 43 72 04 23, open tue-sun 8.30pm-1am, metro alexandre dumas

Shopping

(5) How cool it will be when you tell your friends that you ate the baguette that won the 2001 prize for 'Best Baguette in Paris'. **Boulangerie Au 140** also offers delicious chicken or vegetarian (herbs-avocado) sandwiches for a mere €3.

140 rue de belleville, 20th arr, telephone (01) 46 36 92 47, open mon-thu 12am-2pm & 7pm-11pm, fri 12am-2pm & 7.30pm-midnight, sat 7.30pm-midnight, price lunch €13, diner €18, metro pyrénées

(15) Red, red, red! **Nº 44-II** project, the 'must-visit' Japanese store. It is a new type of concept shop, mixing brand-new trends from creators all around the world. Their original line is designed in their atelier in Paris. Have a look!

59 rue jean-pierre timbaud, 11th arr, telephone (01) 56 98 18 44, open mon-sat 12am-8pm, metro parmentier

(16) Young Austrian designer **Sissi Holleis** has worked in fashion houses headed by Karl Lagerfeld, Guy Laroche and Jean Colonna. The like-named boutique, in black lacquer and reflecting mirrors replete with an oversized chandelier, is a favorite among groovy Parisians. You'll find shoes by Italian designers Quelle and Japanese shoe-designers AKA, together with jewelry by ANN and Yoshiko Design.

3 rue de Nemours, 11th arr, telephone (01) 43 38 10 71, open mon-sat 11am-7pm, metro parmentier

(17) **A Raya San'system** has already been operating for many years, selling parts of old designer collections at discount prices. Get lucky and pull together a 'flashy' designer ensemble. A good place to find an outfit for a night out on the town.

14 rue ternaux, 11th arr, telephone (01) 40 21 74 29, open tue-sat 12am-8pm, sun 3pm-7pm, metro parmentier

(18) **La Botica** is a space for creative exposure, making it possible for young designers to present their work: furniture, jewels, clothes… The store puts its customers directly in contact with the creators, who pay frequent visits. *116 rue saint-maur, 11th arr, telephone (01) 43 55 55 16, open mon 2pm-8pm, tue-sat 12am-8pm, metro parmentier*

(19) **Africouleur** is a unique shop offering an original clothing collection (ladies' dresses, skirts, shoes, scarves, hats, kids' clothes) and household linens, produced from traditional textiles (wax, bazin...) with a trendy western spin. They also have a website from which you can order other items you may not find in the shop (*www.africouleur.com*). *108-110 rue saint-maur, 11th arr, telephone (01) 56 98 15 36, open mon-sat 10.30am-10.30pm, metro saint-maur*

(20) **L'Autoécole** has funky accessories such as furry purses, wiry necklaces and a myriad of 'objets'. Looking for the ultimate 'one-of-a-kind' gift? This kitschy store will surely deliver. *101 rue oberkampf, 11th, telephone (01) 43 55 31 94, open tue-sun 12am-8.30pm, metro ménilmontant*

(21) In keeping with the 'attitude' of Ménilmontant, **La Ruelle** is a tiny store with a purple window, offering an attractive mix of original clothing, shoes, jewels and objects d'art…You'll even be delighted to find a small second-hand area at the back. Fantastic! *130 rue oberkampf, 11th arr, telephone (01) 48 06 71 50, open daily 12am-midnight, metro ménilmontant*

(29) It's not the most famous, but in my opinion, the **Marché Aux Puces de Montreuil** is the most representative in Paris of how a flea market should be. Parisians who don't want to fight the crowds of the other big flea market at Clignancourt go here. This is also where I bought my cheap bicycle! *avenue de la porte de montreuil, 20th arr, sat-mon 7am-7.30pm, metro porte de montreuil*

⑤ BOULANGERIE AU 140

Nice to do

⑥ After serving time as an abandoned industrial building inhabited by squatters, **Le Théâtre de Fortune** now serves as a performing arts space where young dancers, actors and artists can express themselves. Call for program and opening hours.
12 rue de l'ermitage, 20the arr, telephone (01) 43 49 39 66, metro pyrénées

⑭ **Le Berry-Zèbre** was the only cinema in the district. It closed in 1995, in spite of collaborative efforts to maintain it, but after eight years, Francis Schoeller (a man from the circus world) repurchased it. Re-opened in 2002, it is now a multicultural performance space.
63 boulevard de belleville, 20th arr, reservations (01) 43 55 55 55, metro couronnes

Belleville & Ménilmontant

From the Colonel Fabien metro, walk along boulevard de la Vilette to café Le Galopin ① on Place Sainte-Marthe, for a delicious breakfast. Energized enough to climb Paris' highest hill? Walk back to boulevard de la Vilette, via rue Burnouf, through avenue Simon Bolivar to rue Georges Lardennois ②, and enjoy the spectacular view. After a few meters, you'll arrive at the quaint Parc des Buttes Chaumont ③. Go along avenue de la Cascade to the Mouzaïa neighborhood ④, with all of its cool houses. Walk through rue Arthur Rozier to rue de Belleville 140 ⑤ for a tasty baguette. Next make your way down rue de Jourdain to the heart of Belleville, along a small part of rue des Pyrénées, right on to rue Levert to rue des Cascades. Here stands the famous Théâtre de Fortune ❻ and the Regards ⑦. Back via rue de Couronne to rue de Transvaal, you'll approach Villa Castel ⑧. Go to the end on the right for a well-deserved rest at Rital et Courts ⑨, or walk to the top of Parc de Belleville ⑩ ⑪. Exit the park on the north side and go along rue de Belleville towards the Asian district ⑫ ⑬. Maurice Chevalier described Ménilmontant as 'calm', 'sweet' and 'poetic'. The spirit of the village remains. Now visit the multicultural center Berry Zèbre ❶❹ whose doors have been open to the public for eight years. Here, right on boulevard de la Vilette, around rue Oberkampf, find an array of popular shops - some trendy, others selling wonderful accessories ⑮ ⑯ ⑰ ⑱ ⑲ ⑳ ㉑. Rue Oberkampf is also known for its many cafés ㉒. In fact, this may well be the hippest neighborhood in the city! After the shops, visit the home of Edith Piaf ㉓. When you get hungry, head for the affordable La Boulangerie ㉔ or, if you lack a reservation, to one of the other restaurants in the area ㉕ ㉖. Further on, pass through the famous Père Lachaise ㉗ cemetery. To end the day with a bang, stop off at La Flèche d'Or ㉘ where you can dance the night away. The next morning, on avenue de la Porte de Montreuil you'll find the Marché Aux Puces de Montreuil ㉙.

1. Le Galopin
2. Rue Georges Lardennois
3. Parc des Buttes Chaumonts
4. Mouzaïa
5. Boulangerie Au 140
6. Le Théâtre de Fortune
7. Regards
8. Villa Castel
9. Rital et Courts
10. Parc de Belleville
11. Maison de l'Air
12. Chez Ramona
13. Aux Folies
14. Le Berry-Zèbre
15. N°44-II
16. Sissi Holleis
17. A Raya San'system
18. La Botica
19. Africouleur
20. L'Autoécole
21. La Ruelle
22. Café Charbon
23. Musée Edith Piaf
24. Le Soleil
25. Lou Pascalou
26. La Boulangerie
27. Père Lachaise
28. La Flèche d'Or
29. Marché Aux Puces de Montreuil

○ Sights
○ Food & drink
○ Shopping
● Nice to do

La Goutte d'Or & Montmartre

Travel to the north of Paris, to the 18th arrondissement, to enjoy two different sides of the 'city of lights': La Goutte d'Or and Montmartre. La Goutte d'Or is the heart of 'African Paris'. The majority of the people walking on the streets are black or Arab. Exotic colors and aromas abound. Unfortunately the media tends to portray this neighborhood as the headquarters of dealers, prostitutes and pickpockets. Don't believe the hype! The area is truly unique, and you cannot miss it. Montmartre, on the contrary, is the place to live. Topped by the famous Church of Sacré Coeur, this ancient quarter has served

as the favored residence of the bohemian world. Until the 20th century, Montmartre had a more rustic look and provided visual fodder for Van Gogh, Pissarro, Utrillo and other artists. Montmartre is also famed for its nightlife; among its many nightclubs is the Moulin Rouge. In the past few years, some new trendy shops have also settled on the hill - making the area even more lively.

9x Musts!

Bistrot au Gamin de Paris

Coffee and a beignet
at Bistrot Au Gamin
de Paris.

La Goutte d'Or en Tati

Shopping at La Goutte
d'Or and Tati.

Café des Deux Moulins

Lunch in
'le Bar d'Amélie'.

Montmartre

Montmartre: the little
streets, the museums
and the vineyard.

Chez Francis

A break at café
Chez Francis.

Sacré Coeur

Le Sacré Cœur and
the spectacular view.

Rue des Abbesses

Shopping on
rue des Abbesses.

Le Restaurant

Dinner at Le Restaurant.

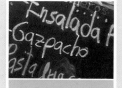

Le Café-Bar Jaune

Le Bar-Café Jaune
for fun.

 Sights
Shopping

 Food & drink
 Nice to do

Sights

(12) It's midnight, and you're in the center of Pigalle. Head towards the **Musée de l'Erotisme** where you'll discover thousands of erotic works. Don't giggle, everything here is art! Worth a visit for its extensive collection of erotic art that includes paintings, sculptures and furniture (!) from all over the world.

72 boulevard de clichy, 18th arr, telephone (01) 42 58 28 73, open daily from 10am-2am, admission €7, metro pigalle

(13) **Place Blanche** is the 'white square'. 'White' because it used to be on the way to Montmartre's plasterer, and the ceaseless traffic of cars, dust-covered with plaster, bleached the roadway. It is here that you'll find the Moulin Rouge.

place blanche, 18th arr, metro blanche

(16) In the 16th century, mills dotted the landscape of this area. Today, one of the last windmills in Paris, **Le Moulin de la Galette**, still stands proudly. Most windmills were destroyed over time.

corner rues girardon and lepic, 18th arr, metro abbesses

(17) Marcel Aymé, a French writer, is an author of fiction novels laced with imagination. His oeuvre includes Le Passe-Muraille and the Contes du Chat Perchét. Here find the sculpture of the **Passe-Muraille**, carried out by Jean Marais, a famous French actor.

place marcel aymé, 18th arr, metro abbesses

(18) The quiet '**Château des Brouillards**' is in front of Renoir's atelier. The castle was built in 1772. In 1846, Gérad de Nerval lived here and considered buying the nearby vineyard. It has been considered one of the most beautiful viewpoints in Paris. On the side of the 'Allée', find the bust of the singer Dalida, who also lived here.

8 allée des brouillards, 18th arr, metro abbesses

(19) Open in 1960, the **Musée de Montmartre** houses the collection of the Society of History and Archaeology, created in 1886. Assembled by scholars, artists and lovers of 'the hill', this collection shows the artistic, political, religious and folk history of this area. Find a replica of the old village, an unequalled collection of Clignancourt Factory Porcelains and a fine collection of posters from the Golden Age of Montmartre.
12 rue cortot, 18th arr, telephone (01) 46 06 61 11, open tue-sun 11am-6pm, admission €4, metro lamarck caulaincourt

(20) **Vineyards** came into to being two thousand years ago in Paris, introduced by the Romans. Regarded as a profitable business, the cultivation of vineyards spread rapidly in the capital. By the 18th century, however, the quality of the productions was very poor, quantity being favored over quality. You still can buy the expensive wine that hails from this vine, but it isn't really worth it.
rue cortot, 18th arr, metro lamarck caulaincourt

(22) **Saint-Pierre de Montmartre** is perhaps the oldest church in Montmartre. Close to the water tower, it stands on rue du Mont-Cenis, a former procession route. The church was built in between 1133 and 1147, and the splendid glass window was made in 1954 by Max Ingrand.
rue du mont-cenis, 18th arr, telephone (01) 46 06 57 63, open daily 8.30am-7pm, metro abbesses

(24) At the **Dalí Museum** you'll find a 'surreal' presentation of about 300 works by artist Salvador Dalí (sculptures, serigraphy…). Special lighting effects and the artist's omnipresent voice-over add to the spectacle. An artist's atelier is also located on the top floor. Outside, one of the best views of Paris.
11 rue poulbot, 18th arr, telephone (01) 42 64 40 10, open daily sept-june 10am-6.30pm, july-aug 10am-9pm, admission €7, metro abbesses

㉕ In 1873, the National Assembly declared its plans to erect **Le Sacré Coeur**, a grand Romano-Byzantine basilica dedicated to the Sacred Heart, intended for public usage. Construction began in 1876 based on the design of Abadie. He intended for it to echo the cathedral of St. Front in Périgueux, which he had restored. Thanks to public donations, the building was completed in 1910 and consecrated in 1919. The interior of the church holds a wealth of treasures: marble sculptures, stained glass windows and mosaics. Standing on the stairs of the Sacré-Coeur, you have a breathtaking panoramic view Paris.
place du parvis du sacré-coeur, 18th arr, telephone (01) 53 41 89 00, metro abbesses

㉖ Located at the foot of Montmartre, the **Musée d'Art Naïf Max Fourny** features temporary exhibitions on varying themes. Shows for children and adults, as well as many art workshops, are held in the auditorium. You'll also find a bar/restaurant where you can browse through newspapers in a relaxing atmosphere.
halle saint-pierre, 2 rue ronsard, 18th arr, telephone (01) 42 58 72 89, open tue-sun 10am-6pm, metro anvers

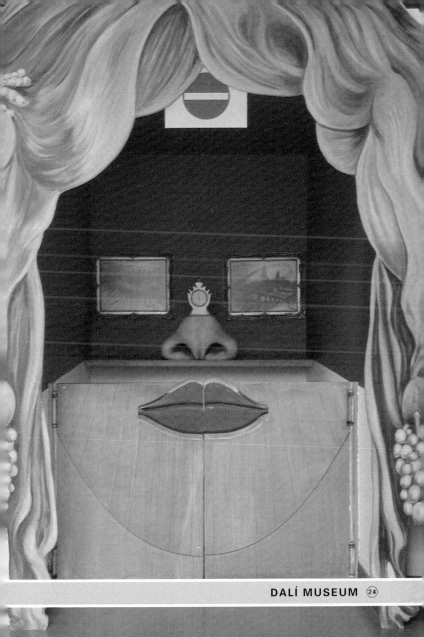

④ **OLYMPIC CAFÉ**

Food & drink

(3) **Bistrot Au Gamin de Paris** is a welcoming bar attractively decorated to give one the impression of dining in the midst of a vineyard. Located in the midst of 'African Paris', its 1clientele is warm and friendly. Don't be surprised to find yourself pulled into conversation or exchanging pleasant smiles with your neighbors. A secret little place… and you'll be the only tourist in the bar!
55 rue doudeauville, 18th arr, telephone 06 11 62 77 65, open 9am-midnight, metro château rouge

(4) **Olympic Café** is trendy, but is, thankfully, still 'unknown'. You must come here on a Thursday night when they host jazz concerts…Enjoy dinner first; the meal is cheap and tasty. It's a bit smoky here, but the friendly owner and waiters are breaths of fresh air.
20 rue léon, 18th arr, telephone (01) 42 52 29 93, open mon-sat 7pm-2am, price menu €12, metro château rouge

(7) **Chez Aida** is just the ticket for those who love authentically African (more specifically Senegalese) food. The restaurant is known for having probably the best theiuboudien (spicy fish stew over rice) in all of Paris. A generous plate and welcoming staff. The prices are easy on the wallet, and you will want to come back!
48 rue polonceau, 18th arr, telephone (01) 42 58 26 20, open thu-tue noon-midnight, price menu €10, metro château rouge

(15) **Café des Deux Moulins** or 'le bar d'Amélie' is located on rue Lepic, one of the most popular market streets in Paris. You may remember it from the recent French film success, Le Fabuleux Destin d'Amélie Poulain. On the café's terrace, order a 'crème brûlée d' Amélie' and coffee, and do as Amélie did and spot animals in the clouds. Can you see the rabbit?
15 rue lepic, 18th arr, telephone (01) 42 54 90 50, open daily 7.30am-10pm, price lunch menu €10, metro blanche

(21) Located on the other side of the hill, **Francis la Butte** is one of the new bars helping to make this area more and more trendy. The atmosphere is relaxing, the waiters friendly. Moreover, it is pleasant to escape the crowded Parisian streets and have a bit of respite.

122 rue caulaincourt, 18th arr, telephone (01) 42 23 58 26, open daily 8am-1am, metro lamarck caulaincourt

(27) It's Friday night and you have no money left, what to do? Eat free cous-cous (the delicious Arabic specialty) at **la Chope du Château Rouge**. Just make sure you're there by 8pm to get a seat. Except for bottles of wine, the drinks are quite cheap.

40 rue de clignancourt, 18th arr, telephone (01) 46 06 20 10, open daily 7am-2am, metro anvers

(31) **Le Sancerre** is the most popular bar in the area. The crowds arrive after 10 pm, so I advise you to try to get a seat on the terrace at about 6pm, order an 'apéro' (try a Ricard) and enjoy your evening.

35 rue des abbesses, 18th arr, telephone (01) 42 58 08 20, open daily 8am-2am, price €10, metro abbesses

(32) To be honest, Montmartre is full of tourists, and subsequently, many bad restaurants. So if you're gonna dine at **Le Restaurant**, make a reservation first. There is an English (and quite poetic) version of the menu 'carte'. I'm a fan of the place, and I advise you to start your meal with a 'chèvre chaud (warm goat cheese)'. For such fine quality, the inexpensive price is unbeatable!

32 rue veron, 18th arr, telephone (01) 42 23 06 22, open daily 12am-3pm & 7.30pm-11.30pm, price menu €20, metro pigalle

(34) **Le Café-Bar Jaune** has a real 'Franco-Spanish' ambiance. Gérard, the man with the long hair and the owner of the place, will be glad to receive you. Ask for a punch or sangria, specialties of the house. There is often a concert on Friday night and interesting exhibitions in the back.

6 rue germain pilon, 18th arr, telephone (01) 42 58 03 05, open daily 7.30pm-2am, metro pigalle

Shopping

(1) **Le marché aux Puces de Saint-Ouen** is the largest and oldest market in Paris, known all over the world! It attracts 150,000 visitors a week. There are a variety of different sub-markets, but too many 'new' products in my opinion. Don't forget: hide your cell phone and beware of pickpockets!
porte de clignancourt, 18th arr, open sat-mon 7am-7.30pm, metro porte de clignancourt

(2) **Marché Dejean** is a spectacle. Women in African 'boubous', some carrying babies on their backs, buying heaps of fish for the evening meal. Little stores displaying stands full of manioc, bananas and ginger, and windows stocked with a variety of black hair- and skin-care products.
rue dejean, 18th arr, open daily 9am-7.30pm, metro château rouge

(5) Live chicks! If you'd like to see something really unique, look through the windows of **Volailles Vivantes**... Kentucky Fried Chicken's got nothing on this place!
42 rue myrha, 18th arr, telephone (01) 46 06 46 04, open daily 9pm-7pm, metro château rouge

(6) For a keepsake to remind you of 'African Paris', I invite you to visit the tiny African art shop called **Afrique Artisana**, where you'll find handbags, necklaces, etc...Note: this is not a 'touristy' shop. You'll see what I mean when you get there.
44-46 rue myrha, 18th arr, open mon-sat 10am-6pm, telephone (01) 42 58 12 13, metro château rouge

(8) You've heard about 'black magic', now see it in practice. Make someone fall in love with you or prepare a death wish. Go to **Kabaco**, the marabou shop! Mysteries abound. Enter only if you believe...or dare.
36 rue polonceau, 18th arr, telephone 06 73 65 06 77, open daily 9am-7.30pm, metro château rouge

(9) **La Rue de la Mode** is the result of a movement to install designers in this area. Rue des Gardes became the first street in Paris to be entirely devoted to fashion and the creations of burgeoning designers. Fourteen young designers have already set up their stores and workshops here, thanks to reduced rents offered by the city.

rue des gardes, 18th arr, metro barbès rochechouart

(10) The **Tati** stores first opened their doors here in 1949. Since then, the shopping kingdom of low low prices has evolved into an empire and is very much a local legend. Other cheap stores like Hand M, however, have encroached on Tati's territory and threaten to muscle it out.

4 boulevard rochechouart, 18th arr, telephone (01) 55 28 50 00, open mon-fri 10am-7pm, sat 9.15am-7pm, metro barbès rochechouart

(28) Everybody seems to agree that the boutique **Omiz** offers a brilliant selection of clothes from the cream of the young new stylists of Paris. You'll also find great accessories like necklaces made with twisted wire. 'Fashionable and sexy.'

8 rue des abbesses, 18th arr, telephone (01) 42 52 13 30, metro abbesses

(29) Few new shops have settled in the short rue Vieuville. You should visit all of them, but I specially recommend you visit **Spree**. It is a cool shop with clothes, jewelry and retro furniture. The place is trendy, but the mood is inviting!

16 rue la vieuville, 18th arr, telephone (01) 42 23 41 40, open tue-sat 11pm-7.30am, metro abbesses

(30) The lively colors and the sexy 'ranch' style of the boutique attract you... **Bonnie Cox** reinforced her fashion-forward reputation when she became the first in Paris to carry the stylish clothes of Xüly Bet. For women's clothing.

38 rue des abbesses, 18th arr, telephone (01) 42 54 95 68, open daily 11am-8pm, metro abbesses

③③ Many talented designers have set up shops in Montmartre, each hoping to achieve instant recognition and success. However, when you visit **Pamp'lune**, hidden on the quiet rue Piémontési, it seems these designers are foregoing commercial success, and instead are just doing their own thing and creating what they love. This is a great address for finding lovely children's clothes.
4 bis rue piémontési, 18th arr, telephone (01) 46 06 50 23, open tue-sat 9.30am-7pm, metro abbesses

Nice to do

⑪ Down the hill, in the middle of a crowded neighborhood, rests **Chez Michou**, the setting of the most famous of 'Transformistes' cabarets in Paris. Everything in the cabaret is blue. See Michou himself, dressed in his favorite suit, a smile spread over his kind face. Make friends - this man belongs to the 'Parisian jet set'.
80 rue des martyrs, 18th arr, telephone (01) 46 06 16 04, open daily 8.30pm-2am, metro pigalle

⑭ **Le Moulin-Rouge** is certainly the best known cabaret in all of Paris and maybe in the world. A restaurant as well as a showcase for dancing girls, it maintains the Cancan tradition accompanied by Offenbach's world-famous tune. Welcome to the window of the 'Parisian gaîtés', made popular by the drawings of Toulouse-Lautrec.
82 boulevard de clichy, place blanche, 18e arr, telephone (01) 53 09 82 82, open shows 9pm & 11pm, price show 9pm €92, show 11pm €82, price diner & show 7pm from €130, metro blanche

㉓ **Place du Tertre** is brimming with souvenir shops, cafés and sketch artists ready to make your portrait.
place du tertre, 18e arr, metro abbesses

La Goutte d'Or & Montmartre

Begin at the flea market ❶ by the Porte de Clignancourt metro. Or, if you're all shopped out, start at the Château Rouge metro in the African district, La Goutte d'Or. Here you can set out on foot to Montmartre. Walk to the Marché Dejean ❷ and check out the exotic products. Try a 'beignet nature' in the bakery at rue des Poissoniers 15 and a coffee at Bistrot Au Gamin de Paris ❸. On route, visit all of the fabric shops on rue des Poissoniers and rue Doudeauville ❹. And if you want to see something really special, stop by rue Myrha 42 ❺ ❻! At rue des Poissoniers 9, find the shop Kata Soldes, renovated from an old movie theater: go in and admire the décor! Continue along rue Polonceau and experience the African sights and sounds ❼ ❽. Next head over to the remarkable 'La Rue de la Mode ❾' and then visit Tati ❿. Set off over boulevard Rochechouart, and walk to the highlights of Pigalle and its sex shops ⓫ ⓬. Eventually arrive at Place Blanche ⓭ ⓮. Now you're entering the heart of Montmartre. Take rue Lepic. If you've seen the film 'Amélie of Montmartre', then you'll recognize the Café des Deux Moulins ⓯ at number 15. Vincent and Theo van Gogh lived on the third floor of rue Lepic 54, from 1886 to 1888. On the way to the top of the hill, just beyond the windmills ⓰, you'll find the sculpture Le Passe-Muraille ⓱ and the Château des Brouillards ⓲. Walk further to rue de Cortot ⓳ ⓴ and don't forget the other side of Montmartre: often overlooked by tourists. Rue Caulaincourt is a cozy street filled with bars. It's the up and coming trendy neighborhood in Paris. Some cafés, such as Francis La Butte ㉑, are excellent spots to take a deserved break. Place du Tertre ㉒ ㉓ ㉔ and Sacré Coeur ㉕ are the most visited sights on Montmartre. Via rue Muller ㉖, you'll reach the multi-faceted Halle Saint-Pierre ㉗. There's loads of shopping on rue Abbesses, with Omiz and Bonnie Cox ㉘ ㉙ ㉚ ㉛ ㉝ ㉞, rue Vieuville and rue Houdon are also must-visits. And this is also where you'll find the excellent Le Restaurant ㉜.

1. Le Marché aux Puces de Saint-Ouen
2. Marché Dejean
3. Bistrot au Gamin de Paris
4. Olympic Café
5. Volailles Vivantes
6. Afrique Artisana
7. Chez Aida
8. Fofana Sekou
9. Rue de la Mode
10. Tati
11. Chez Michou
12. Musée de l'Erotisme
13. Place Blanche
14. Le Moulin-Rouge
15. Café des Deux Moulins
16. Moulin de la Galette
17. Passe-Muraille
18. Château des Brouillards
19. Musée de Montmartre
20. Vineyards
21. Chez Francis
22. Saint-Pierre de Montmartre
23. Place du Tertre
24. Dalí Museum
25. Le Sacré Coeur
26. Musée d'Art Naïf Max Fourny
27. La Chope du Château Rouge
28. Omiz
29. Spree
30. Bonnie Cox
31. Le Sancerre
32. Le Restaurant
33. Pamp'Lune
34. Le Café-Bar Jaune

● Sights
● Food & drink
● Shopping
● Nice to do

Nightlife

You can find the letters on the general map in the front of the book.

(K) Le Batofar

Every trendspotter, clubber and techno purist is there. The Batofar is a house-boat, and the scene is oriented towards urban lifestyles and urban music. You can listen to great DJs, watch screenings… I like to be there on Sunday afternoons, chilling out in its pleasant lounge atmosphere. Note that some nights are free.

11 quai françois mauriac, 13th arr, telephone (01) 56 29 10 00, open tue-sun midnight-5am, metro quai de la gare

(L) Vip Room

An exclusive nightclub complete with red carpet, a VIP terrace and lots of stars. Well, it has to be said, not everybody can get in. Top three ways to gain entrance: be a star, be a friend of the owner Jean Roch, or probably the easiest, be lucky enough to find an invitation on the street!

76-78 avenue des champs-elysees, 8th arr, telephone (01) 56 69 16 66, open tue-sun 11.30pm-5am, metro george v

(M) Studio des Islettes

A tiny but innovative jazz club in Paris, settled on a dark street in La Goutte d'Or. You'll appreciate the jam sessions, which prove to be wonderful occasions to witness creative exchanges among a variety of musicians. Many jazz ensembles are created here. Jam sessions take place Monday to Thursday. For jazz lovers only.

10 rue des islettes, 18th arr, telephone (01) 42 58 63 33, open daily 8pm-2am, metro barbès rochechouart

(N) Bus Palladium

This hip place, with a particularly long bar, is above all a spot for dancing and having fun. Ladies rule the house at Tuesday's Ladies' Night, with free entrance and free drinks all night long. The music changes during the week, but 'house' pumps all weekend long.

6 rue fontaine, 9th arr, telephone (01) 53 21 07 33, open daily 11pm-6am, metro blanche

(O) Cinéma MK2 Quai De Seine

A modern six-screen movie theater set in an ancient warehouse, just beside the 'Canal de la Villette'. This complex is devoted to European cinema, quiet art movies and short films. All movies are shown in their original version and are preceded by a short film. The most romantic cinema of the city!

14 quai de la seine, 19th arr, telephone (08) 92 68 14 07, metro stalingrad

(P) Le Rex Club

One could say that Rex Club is the trendiest, friendliest club in Paris. Besides Garnier - who won the 'Victoire De La Musique Award' (France's equivalent to the Grammy's) for his album '30' - the Rex Club has featured such famous DJs as: Carl Cox, Daft Punk, Deep, Jeff Mills, Kevin Saunderson and Sven Vath. Great!

1 boulevard poissonnière, 2nd arr, telephone (01) 42 36 83 93, open wed-sat 11.30pm-7am, metro bonne-nouvelle

(Q) L'Enfer

L'Enfer is well known for it's late late hours. Don't be surprised to see hip boys and girls arriving at 5am...They've just come from the Queen and can't stop grooving to the house/techno beat. The club attracts a gay clientele - just like all the best places in Paris.

34 rue de départ, 15th arr, telephone (01) 42 79 94 53, open thu-sun 11.30pm-6am + 'after hours' until 10am, metro montparnasse bienvenue

(R) Les Bains

Once a Turkish bath, Les Bains is the place to see and be seen. The dance floor is pretty small, the décor is a bit disappointing, but still, with its throbbing 'house' music, Les Bains stays the emblematic place to meet models and celebrities!

7 rue du bourg-l'abbé, 3rd arr, telephone (01) 48 87 01 80, open daily 11.30pm-6am, metro strasbourg st denis

(S) Banana Café

Le Banana Café offers high spirits and a great party. It is renowned for its mix of clientele - all night birds. There is a street-level bar and go-go dancers. The basement has another atmosphere: in its more intimate space, you'll find a dance floor featuring a live pianist accompanied by recorded music.

13 rue de la ferronnerie, 1st arr, telephone (01) 42 33 35 31, open daily 4pm-7am, metro châtelet

GEORGES

More sights

You can find the letters on the general map in the front of the book.

Ⓣ Cimetière Montmartre

This cemetery became the site of huge mass graves after the siege of the Commune in 1871. It serves as the final resting place of writer Alexandre Dumas, composer Hector Berlioz, and many other artistic luminaries. Émile Zola was also buried here until his corpse was moved to the Panthéon in 1908.
20 avenue rachel, 18th arr, telephone (01) 43 87 64 24, open daily 8am-5.30pm, metro place de clichy of blanche

Ⓤ Musée Rodin

You can visit the museum building and its beautiful gardens separately. The museum contains various works as well as Rodin's personal collection. The gardens are dotted with sculptures, including 'The Burghers of Calais' and 'The Gates of Hell.'
77 rue de varenne, 7th arr, telephone (01) 44 18 61 10, open tue-sun apr-sep 9.30am-5.45pm (gardens until 6.45pm), oct-mar 9.30am-4.45pm (gardens 5pm), admission €5 (gardens €1), métro varenne or rer invalides

Ⓥ La Défense

The name 'défense' originates from the monument La Défense de Paris, which was erected on this site in 1883 in commemoration of the War of 1870. The project to build the Grande Arche was initiated by former French president Mitterand, who envisioned a 20th century version of the Arc de Triomphe. Danish architect Otto van Spreckelsen's design consists of a 106-meter-tall white building with the middle portion left open. The sides of the cube contain offices. You can take an elevator to the top of the Arche de la Défense, where you'll be rewarded with a nice view of the city center, just over two miles away.
1 parvis de la défense, telephone (01) 49 07 27 57, open summer 9am-8pm, winter 9am-7pm, métro grande arche de la défense

(w) Cimetière Montparnasse

Hiding in the shadow of the modern Tour Montparnasse lies the beautiful
Cimetière Montparnasse, opened in 1824 as the burial grounds for the Rive
Gauche's most famous residents. The cemetery is the final resting place of
Guy de Maupassant, Sartre, De Beauvoir, and Samuel Beckett.
3 boulevard edgar quinet, 14th arr, telephone (01) 44 10 86 50, open 15
mar-oct mon-fri 8am-6pm, sat 8.30am-6pm, sun and holidays 9am-6pm,
nov-15 mar mon-fri 8am-5.30pm, sat 8.30am-5.30pm, métro edgar quinet

(x) Canal Saint-Martin

There is quite a bit of romance surrounding the Canal Saint-Martin! Created
during the Restoration period from 1821 to 1825, the canal is almost three
miles long. There is also a system of locks in order to compensate the
water levels, as the difference is over 25 yards.
canal saint-martin, 10th arr, métro louis blanc or jaurès

(y) Village Saint-Paul

The village was created when the area was renovated, and this is a maze
of courtyards on different levels, entirely occupied by galleries, libraries,
antique shops, and a few cafés. Loitering is a delight here, as this is like
a village in the middle of the city, located between the Quai des Celestins,
rue St Paul, and rue Charlemagne. The area is 'protected' from the outside
world by houses surrounding the village, and here you'll find more than 60
antique dealers and outlets.
village saint-paul, 4th arr, open daily 11am-7pm, métro saint-paul

(z) Place du Marché Sainte-Catherine

The Place du Marché Sainte-Catherine is actually a small island and some-
what of a haven for pedestrians in the Marais. This peaceful square owes
its name to a convent, which was destroyed in 1783. Come rain or shine,
the place is definitely full of romance!
place du marché sainte-catherine, 3rd arr, métro saint-paul

Alphabetical index

Category index

FLORÈS

This guide has been compiled with the utmost care. mo' media bv cannot
be held liable in the case of any inaccuracies within the text. Any remarks
or comments should be directed to the following address.

mo' media, attn. 100% paris,
p.o. box 7028, 4800 ga, breda, the netherlands, e-mail info@momedia.nl

author	franck sabattier
final editing	taunya renson-martin, simon jones,
	alex tobin@burotexture.
photography	marieke hüsstege, duncan de fey
graphic design	www.studio100procent.nl, naarden
cartography	eurocartografie, hendrik-ido-ambacht
project guidance	joyce enthoven & sasja lagendijk, mo' media
printing office	brepols, turnhout (b)

100% paris	isbn 90 5767 098 4 - nur 510, 512
	© mo' media, breda, the netherlands, april 2003